Race and Gender

EQUAL OPPORTUNITIES POLICIES IN EDUCATION

The Open University

This reader is one part of an Open University integrated teaching system and the selection is therefore related to other material available to students. It is designed to evoke the critical understanding of students. Opinions expressed in it are not necessarily those of the course team or of the University.

Race and Gender

EQUAL OPPORTUNITIES POLICIES IN EDUCATION

A Reader edited by

MADELEINE ARNOT

at the Open University

PERGAMON PRESS

OXFORD · NEW YORK · TORONTO · SYDNEY · FRANKFURT

in association with

THE OPEN UNIVERSITY

U.K.	Pergamon Press Ltd., Headington Hill Hall, Oxford OX3 0BW, England
U.S.A.	Pergamon Press Inc., Maxwell House, Fairview Park, Elmsford, New York 10523, U.S.A.
CANADA	Pergamon Press Canada Ltd., Suite 104, 150 Consumers Road, Willowdale, Ontario M2J 1P9, Canada
AUSTRALIA	Pergamon Press (Aust.) Pty. Ltd., P.O. Box 544, Potts Point, N.S.W. 2011, Australia
FEDERAL REPUBLIC OF GERMANY	Pergamon Press GmbH, Hammerweg 6, D-6242 Kronberg-Taunus, Federal Republic of Germany

Selection and editorial material
copyright © 1985 The Open University

First edition 1985

Library of Congress Cataloging in Publication Data

Main entry under title:
Race and gender.
1. Educational equalization—Great Britain—Addresses, essays, lectures. 2. Discrimination in education—Great Britain—Addresses, essays, lectures. I. Arnot, Madeleine.
LC213.3.G7R32 1985   370.19′34′0941   85-9418

British Library Cataloguing in Publication Data

Race and gender: equal opportunities policies in education: a reader.
1. Education equalization—Great Britain
I. Arnot, Madeleine   II. Open University
370′.941   LC213.3.G7

ISBN 0-08-032675-7 Hardcover
ISBN 0-08-032674-9 Flexicover

Printed in Great Britain by A. Wheaton & Co, Ltd., Exeter

Preface

This reader consists of a collection of articles which form part of the Open University Course E333, *Policy-making in Education.* The course critically examines ways of analysing education policy, discusses the structure and process of education policy-making in central and local government, and analyses educational policy in practice through case studies of particular policy issues.

The primary concern of this reader is the analysis of race and gender education policies and programmes for change. Because the reader forms only one part of the course (much of which consists of written texts or broadcasts discussing issues raised in the Reader articles), it cannot claim to offer a complete picture of education policy-making. The selection of articles has been made with the overall course content in mind. It has been designed to highlight specific problems, and to develop the students' critical understanding. Opinions expressed within articles are, therefore, not necessarily those of the course team nor of the university. However, the editor believes that the selection, though not comprehensive, focuses on major issues in education policy-making, and will be useful to anyone with an interest in the area of race and gender.

There are three other readers, also published by Pergamon Press, and related to case studies of education policy which we discuss in course material. These readers are:

Policy-making in Education: the breakdown of consensus. Edited by I. McNay and J. Ozga.

Curriculum and Assessment: some policy issues. Edited by P. Raggatt and G. Weiner.

Education, Training and Employment: towards a new vocationalism? Edited by R. Dale.

* It is not necessary to become an undergraduate of the Open University in order to study the course of which this reader is part. Further information about the course associated with this book may be obtained by writing to: The Admissions Office, The Open University, PO Box 48, Walton Hall, Milton Keynes MK7 6AB.

Contents

Introduction

The articles in this reader are selected to complement Open University course material[1]* that focuses on the patterns of race and gender inequalities in education and on the methods which have been chosen to tackle such inequalities by central and local government and education institutions. The analyses of race and gender in education represent two different, though complementary, case studies of education policy-making and of the usefulness of different perspectives for understanding education policies. By studying race and gender alongside each other, we can also begin to assess the similarities and differences in the treatment of two structures of social inequality at various levels of education provision. The material in this book contributes to that analysis by offering a range of perspectives on education policy and innovation which are currently available amongst those studying race and gender relations in education. The reader is characterized, therefore, more by the diversity of approaches presented than by a consensus of views.

In putting together this collection I am aware that it would be easy to assume that race and gender are somehow a 'natural pair' of policy problems, since they have been subjected to similar treatment through the establishment of anti-discrimination legislation and its agencies—the Commission for Racial Equality and the Equal Opportunities Commission. For policymakers, the needs of ethnic minorities or women may be perceived as similar 'special cases' within the overall pattern of education provision. For the left, both may be viewed as subordinate layers of inequality within class relations. For teachers and school managers, the issues of race and gender may now be placed together as equally troublesome areas demanding attention. Other more academic parallels may also be drawn pointing to the similarities of race and gender as socially constructed categories premised upon concepts of 'natural' or biological differences.[2]

Such attempts at establishing parallels between race and gender and between the demands of the 'black' movement and the women's movement for educational reform, however, are seen by some as a 'mere academic exercise'. The search for such parallels makes it impossible to understand the combined effect of race and gender inequality experienced by black women.

*Superscript numbers refer to Notes at end of the article.

1

Further, any similarities between the two sets of power relations mask the relation between what has been criticized as essentially a 'white women's movement' and the maintenance of race inequality in British society. Another problem arises when multicultural curriculum materials are developed which are sex biased. More significantly, critics of such attempts to find parallels between race and gender point to the necessity of recognizing that each structure has been affected by different sets of social institutions, has had a different history and therefore requires different forms of analysis.[3]

Obviously this reader cannot solve such theoretical and political problems. However, it can move such debates forward by, at the very least, bringing together material on the policy implications and treatment of the two areas and by introducing such debates into the sphere of policy analysis and institutional studies where often there is little coverage of the issues and few connections made between the two. The material presented here also gives those involved in gender and education the chance to observe the political lessons to be learnt from policy-making in the area of race and ethnicity in education; for those whose special interest has been the policy needs of ethnic minorities, the articles in the second section of the book will illuminate a range of perspectives on policy formation and innovation used to create equal opportunities for women. Specific examples of how in practice links exist between race and gender in the development of anti-discrimination legislation, local authority policy-making on equal opportunities and the demand for single sex schools can be found in the articles by M. Rendel, H. Taylor and S. Tomlinson (Chapters 6, 9, 5 respectively).

Any analysis of the relationship between these two controversial and sensitive policy areas will recognize how debates around race and gender have transformed and utilized the equal opportunity debate that, since the Second World War, provided the basis for a broad consensus of political opinion and educational development. Until the 1970s the concept of equal educational opportunity was used predominantly to analyse social class differences in education. By the end of that decade it seems to have been overtaken by the new rhetoric of vocationalism, with education required to meet the needs of industry and its stratified and differentially skilled work force. Yet surprisingly within the same period the concept of equality of opportunity was put into service again, this time extended to those other disadvantaged groups which had been neglected to some extent by previous 'egalitarian' policies—women, blacks and, more recently, homosexuals and the disabled. So successful has the campaign been to establish special treatment for such groups that some trade unions and local authorities have now recruited 'equal opportunity' officers and advisers. Despite the criticisms of the late 1970s, which pointed to the failure of education to alleviate social inequality, equality of opportunity still seems a viable concept, especially among teachers who see its provision as part of their professional practice. Thus, although the forms of implementation of equal opportunity policies for race and gender might differ in practice, the political rhetoric and thrust of pressure groups can be seen as part of the same normative movement of change.

The case for designing equal opportunity policies in education for gender and race has been strengthened by the presence, though not the use, of anti-discrimination legislation (the Sex Discrimination Act, 1975, and the Race Relations Act, 1976), which included education in its remit. However, there has been some debate about how to define the direction that policy initiatives should take. Strong divisions between policy-makers and among pressure groups can now be found in the area of race, for example between 'anti-racists' and 'multi-culturalists'—that this division is not merely a matter of degree is well demonstrated by Jeffcoate's chapter in this volume (see Chapter 4).

In contrast, instructive parallels with the history of policy-making relating to social class equality of opportunity can be made with gender, where a broad consensus came under increasing strain as the concept of equality of opportunity moved from what Crosland called 'weak' to 'strong' definitions, from equality of access to positive discrimination. The distinction drawn by Weiner[4] between anti-sexist 'feminists' and 'egalitarians' is similar to that 'strong' and 'weak' distinction. While there may be broad agreement about the means, there is conflict about the ends. 'Feminists' and 'egalitarians' both argue that equality of access as promoted by legislation has made little impact on girls' school subject choices or their choice of occupation. Both suggest that more positive policy initiatives are required which would implement not just the letter but the spirit of the law. Such policies would challenge stereotypical views of 'feminine' roles and female employment. Both 'egalitarians' and 'feminists' favour policies which would discriminate positively in favour of girls and which would attempt to change attitudes.

The differences between these two positions, unlike the anti-racist/multi-cultural split, are over short- or long-term goals, over the scope of education policy and its capacity to respond to the need to reduce gender inequality in society. Many 'feminists' support 'egalitarian' policies, and some 'egalitarians', even in relatively powerful positions within government agencies, would see themselves as anti-sexist. The consensus about the need for policy initiatives in this area can unite pressure groups and official and quasi-official bodies such as the Equal Opportunities Commission and the Women's National Commission within the Cabinet Office. Increasingly, HM Inspectorate have also taken the initiative of investigating and proposing change in the area of gender inequality[5] in ways that are not dissimilar to LEA and school programmes. The divisions between those promoting equality of opportunity for women, sex equality and anti-sexist policies are therefore often more a matter of degree than of political opposition.

Since the area of gender equality is a relatively recent arrival on the policy front, it has, as yet, received little attention from policy analysts. There is no available academic critique of 'feminist' or 'egalitarian' initiatives in education which would parallel Jeffcoate's critique of anti-racism. That is not to say that the policy initiatives described in the second section of this reader are widely accepted—there is a strong body of opinion in wider society which regards such policies as coercive, contrary to freedom of choice and restrictive of individual liberty, and contrary to long established patterns of social organization. Sensitivity to the strength of public and professional opinion is something which has affected the shape of policy in the Schools Council Sex Differentiation Project, local authority initiatives and school-based projects, as described in Chapters 8, 9 and 10. Such descriptions of the strategies used for implementing anti-discrimination policies and the problems of innovation are useful resource materials for case studies of policy change. As such, those articles perform a different function from the terse academic analysis of policy debates on race in the first section of this volume.

Turning now to the first section, we can find the variety of contentious viewpoints which reflect the differences between anti-racists and multiculturalists which were referred to earlier.

In the first chapter Andrew Dorn looks at the role of the Race Relations Act (1976) in education and the concepts of direct and indirect discrimination. He shows that not only is the law difficult to use because of its cumbersome procedures but also because of its ambiguous wording. The law has been largely ignored by both multiculturalists and those concerned with 'institutional racism' in schools. Therefore, the full significance of the way in which the concept of discrimination and definitions of equal opportunity had developed in the 1970s by referring to discriminatory structures and processes, he argues, has not been fully understood and could be utilized to greater effect.

An analysis of the role of the DES in responding to what he called the 'racial tinderbox' is provided by David L. Kirp in an extract from his book *Doing Good by Doing Little*.[6] The title summarizes his interpretation of the confusion and ambiguity of the DES's response to the problems of multiracial schools and the poor academic performance of some ethnic minorities. Kirp understands the various policy statements produced by the DES in the context of what was administratively possible for central government, given the terms of the 1944 Education Act. He also points to the dilemma faced by politicians and education officials in developing any notion of positive discrimination for specific groups when the dominant values were those of universalism and consensual decision-making. The result of such restrictions, he argues, was a policy of 'racial inexplicitness'.

Chris Mullard in Chapter 3 argues that the pattern of response by educationalists and the government since the 1960s to the problem of immigration and the education of black pupils in British schools has been one of maintaining stability and control. He argues that it was neither pragmatism nor the choice of proceeding by 'stealth' in order to do good that motivated the DES; rather it was the desire to support the existing structure of society, based upon both capitalist and racist principles. In this controversial analysis he puts forward the view that, despite the apparent differences between the three phases of 'assimilation', 'integration' and 'cultural pluralism', such educational ideals were in fact variations of the same theme. Each expected a degree of cultural change on the part of black groups, and all protected the dominant white interests in society.

In direct contrast with Mullard's perspective, Robert Jeffcoate, in an extract from his recent book *Ethnic Minorities and Education*, presents another controversial critique focusing on what he calls the 'anti-racist' ideology.[7] Such an ideology, he suggests, has manifested itself in a variety of educational issues, particularly within schools. Looking at some examples of the policy implications of this ideology, Jeffcoate argues that as an ideology anti-racism runs counter to liberal and democratic ideals. He is particularly concerned about the effects on teacher autonomy, the quality of school materials and the freedom of pupils to express their views in school.

Finally, a very different approach to the nature of education provision and the problems of relating a minority culture to that of the majority is discussed by Sally Tomlinson in Chapter 5. Here she describes the 'black education' movement and in particular the different forms of supplementary and segregated schools that have been set up by various communities for themselves. Increasingly, she suggests, local authorities will have the problem of deciding what to do about such education provision, especially since the recent stance by the Conservative Government encourages self-help and more parental involvement in education.

The second section, 'Sex Discrimination and Educational Change', raises a different set of questions. For example, does the structure of British educational government impede or facilitate change in education provision to combat gender inequality? Are initiatives in the area of gender the product of national or local pressure groups? Are they a result of legislative change or grass roots activism? What options are open to education advisers, teachers and researchers to raise awareness of the problems of gender differentiation in education and to find solutions? What structural factors within the education service would a programme for equality of opportunity need to take account of? Each of the authors in this section participated in the events she describes—we are thus privileged to gain an 'insider's' view of how various strategies and goals were chosen at various levels of the education system.

The first article in this section, by Margherita Rendel, shows how and why the Sex Discrimination Act was won in 1975 and how the inclusion of education was opposed. Her account reveals the processes involved in achieving policy change through political parties and parliamentary procedures and how, in order to gain legitimacy as an item on the political agenda, compromises had to be made. For those who fought for such legislation, the promise was of national recognition of the problems which women face, and of effective tools for ensuring social change.

In contrast with this view, we find in Eileen Byrne's chapter on 'Equality or Equity?' a very explicit concern at the failure of policy-makers in the United Kingdom to develop 'a coherent national plan for the achievement of educational equality'. In this piece she describes how various European nations have responded to pressure for programmes designed to move towards greater equality of the sexes and how the structure of the U.K. education service, with its lack of accountability, has uniquely abrogated 'its responsibility to ensure a national system of minimum education which incorporates sex equality...'.

Further discussion about the ways in which educational reform can be developed is found in Gaby Weiner's analysis of the Schools Council Sex Differentiation Project. This project is interesting because of the way it became established and the sorts of strategies it adopted. The model of teacher workshops and of giving support to teachers already interested and committed to innovation and 'raising awareness' in their own schools had much in common with the programmes developed later by Hazel Taylor, working as an adviser for equal opportunities in an outer London borough. In Chapter 9 she shows how a political initiative can be converted into an educational one, and how a variety of strategies was used by the local authority to encourage change in its schools and in the community.

What comes through from such accounts is how difficult it is to initiate change even at the local level, how important it is to allocate resources and to maintain contact with teachers and schools over a long period of time. Also, especially in the area of sex discrimination, the correct balance between working at the professional or the personal level is difficult to find. As in the area of race, the value of in-service education for school managers and teachers is only just beginning to be realized.

The final article in this section, and the last of the book, is by Alison Kelly, one of the initiators and participants in the GIST (Girls Into Science and Technology) project. This action research project has now been widely publicized and has come to represent, as she points out, a model for other projects within schools. By looking back at the experience and the results of the scheme, Kelly tries to evaluate how innovation can be brought into schools and what were the lessons to be learnt. Her interest in teachers (rather than national or local policy formation) as change agents contrasts with the increasing centralization of educational management and reform.

This collection of readings offers a range of resource material for the study of race and gender and as such I hope it will be useful for those interested not just in the sociology of education, where many of the debates discussed above have taken place, but also in educational management and policy studies.

Notes

1. See Arnot, M. *Race, Gender and Education Policy-making*, E333 Module 4, Open University Press, Milton Keynes, 1986.
2. Carby, H. Schooling in Babylon, in *The Empire Strikes Back*, Centre for Contemporary Cultural Studies, Hutchinson, London, 1982.
3. I have drawn these points from Hazel Carby, Schooling in Babylon and White women listen! Black feminism and the boundaries of sisterhood, in *The Empire Strikes Back*, op. cit.; and Multi-Culture, *Screen Education*, Spring 1980, No. 34, pp. 62–70.
4. Weiner, G. Feminist education or equal opportunities: the tension within, in Whyte, J., Cruikshank, M., Deem, R., and Kant, L. (eds.), *Girl Friendly Schooling*, Methuen, London, 1985.
5. Orr, P. Sex bias in schools, national perspectives, paper presented at 'Girl Friendly' Schooling Conference, held at Manchester Polytechnic, 1984.
6. Kirp, D.L. *Doing Good by Doing Little*, University of California Press, Berkeley, 1979.
7. Jeffcoate, R. *Ethnic Minorities and Education*, Harper & Row, London, 1984.

Perspectives on Race and Education Policy

1

Education and the Race Relations Act

ANDREW DORN

In the now considerable body of literature on multiracial education there is hardly any mention of the Race Relations Act, 1976. In the debate about racial equality in education, discussion of the relevant legislation is conspicuous by its absence. In academic works on multiculturalism in education, the concept of discrimination appears to have vanished: usually it is not even in the index. Even the anti-racist vanguard, rightly concerned to add some substance to the concept of 'institutionalized racism', with few exceptions, have eschewed any reference to legal formulations as a possible source of clarification of the racism they seek to combat. Is the Race Relations Act irrelevant then to educational policy-making, provision and practice?

At least one experienced LEA adviser, and former chair of the Caribbean Teacher Association, appears to think not. Gerry Davis has argued that:

> Black people do not want any favours or privileges from education authorities. What they want is to be accorded their statutory rights under the law of the land. If the officers, advisers, inspectors, headteachers and teachers in multiracial areas paid serious attention to their statutory obligations under the education acts and anti-discrimination laws, there would be no need for separate policies...anti-discriminatory Acts already embody the policy on which they can identify their professional duty.[1]

To what extent then can the Race Relations Act contribute to the multiracial debate and, following Davis, help teachers and administrators 'identify their professional duty'? What follows is an attempt to use the law in a positive way, as a guide to identifying possible forms of discrimination in education. It must be stressed at the outset that many of the examples given are speculative and hypothetical rather than judgements handed down by the courts. My purpose is not so much a legal exegesis as an attempt to use the concepts of the law in an imaginative way to illuminate the possible racial

Specially commissioned for this volume, © 1985 The Open University.

consequences of educational practices; the focus is as much on the spirit of the law as the letter of the law.

DISCRIMINATION

Central to the Race Relations Act is its definition of racial discrimination. Two types of discrimination are identified, direct and indirect. Direct discrimination, section 1(1)(a), occurs when a person treats another 'less favourably' on 'racial grounds'. An overt example of this is provided by the Bristol primary school teacher who subjected a black colleague to taunts such as:

> Here comes the foreigner. Wogs, pakis, coons, they're all the same to me. All wogs should go back to wogland. I'm a racist you know.[2]

Direct discrimination need not be as obvious as the above, one hopes isolated, example. For instance, it is not necessary to show that the person openly expressed an intention to discriminate, it is sufficient to be able to infer discrimination from the particular circumstances. A number of commentators though stress the importance of establishing a discriminatory motive. Thus Macdonald suggests that:

> What matters under this definition is the reason or reasons for the discrimination . . . direct discrimination is limited to cases where a discriminatory motive may be inferred.[3]

On the other hand, the Commission for Racial Equality (CRE) have argued that direct discrimination need not be deliberate and that the motivation of the discriminator is not a relevant consideration.[4]

If the Commission's interpretation is correct, then the concept of direct discrimination could be illuminating in looking at various instances of teacher expectations and treatment of pupils according to their race. For instance, in their study of a Yorkshire comprehensive school, Carrington and Wood[5] claimed that many teachers perceived black pupils as having 'skills of the body rather than skills of the mind' which resulted in their being channelled into sporting rather than academic pursuits. The whole issue of teacher stereotypes of pupil aptitudes and potentialities based on racial (not to mention class and gender) assumptions is a sensitive one, but it is not far-fetched to assume that it might result in 'less favourable treatment' on 'racial grounds'.

Altogether more complicated, yet potentially more fruitful in examining educational practices, is the law's definition of indirect discrimination, section 1(1)(b) of the Act. Indirect discrimination occurs when a 'requirement or condition' is applied equally to all, but a 'considerably smaller' proportion of a particular racial group 'can comply' with it, compared to persons who are not of that racial group; that the requirement is not 'justifiable' and that failure to comply with it is 'detrimental'. In simple language, indirect discrimination extends the notion of discrimination to include rules, procedures and criteria that have a discriminatory *effect* regardless of their motive or intention. It allows us to consider taken-for-granted conventions and practices, ostensibly not racial at all but which have racial consequences in terms of whom they exclude and affect. For instance, in education, school rules regarding uniform, church schools' admissions criteria or English language qualifications for entry to certain courses, whilst not in themselves racial, nor so intended, might nonetheless have the effect of excluding disproportionate numbers of persons from particular racial groups. The key issues in law are the terms 'considerably smaller', 'can comply', 'detriment' and 'justifiable', all of which have been the subject of interpretation in cases and legal opinion. For instance, does 'justifiable' mean 'reasonable', 'necessary', 'essential', 'tolerable'?[6] When local education authorities (LEAs) advertise senior administrative posts and stipulate previous experience of educational administration as an essential requirement, is this 'justifiable', since very few black people will have had such experience?

Before speculating further on the considerable possibilities of applying the concept of indirect discrimination to educational settings it would be useful to turn to an actual, and important, case as an illustration, that of *Mandla* vs. *Dowell-Lee*. In 1978 Mr Mandla wanted to enter his son, Gurinder, at Park Grove, a private school in Birmingham. As a Sikh, Gurinder was refused entry to the school because he was unable to comply with the school uniform rules, i.e. that he should remove his turban. At first, the courts found against the Mandlas on the grounds that the no turban rule was justifiable, that Gurinder 'could comply' (i.e. could physically remove his turban) and that anyway Sikhs were a religious not a racial or ethnic group. Eventually (1983) the Mandlas' appeal came to the House of Lords, who ruled in their favour on the grounds that 'can comply' meant 'can in practice comply' or can comply 'consistently with the customs and cultural conditions' of the racial group in question. Furthermore, their Lordships held that the school's uniform rule (no turbans) was not justifiable (on educational grounds) and that, after all, Sikhs were a racial group. This last point raised by the Mandla case is important and requires some explanation. It raises the question of what in law is an ethnic/racial group?

RACIAL GROUP

Section 3 of the Race Relations Act, 1976, defines a racial group by reference to 'colour, race, nationality or ethnic or national origins'. This would appear to be sufficiently broad to cover all groups liable to experience discrimination, but the definition does not include religion[7], nor does it say by whom the group is defined (is my own subjective ethnic identity sufficient?). Consequently, until the House of Lords' ruling there were doubts about whether Jews, Sikhs and Gypsies constituted racial groups within the meaning of the law. The Lords have now laid down a more objective checklist for determining racial group.[8] Essential characteristics are said to be 'a long shared history' and a 'cultural tradition of its own'. Furthermore, a number of other features are likely to be present: a common geographic origin (or descent from a small number of common ancestors), a common language, a common literature, a common religion and being either a minority or a majority within a larger community. Additionally, the Lords said that a person was a member of a racial group if he/she considered him/herself a member and was accepted as such. Whilst this is altogether more comprehensive, one still wonders how, for instance, Rastafarians would be treated by the law.

EDUCATION

Several sections of the Act refer specifically to education. Section 17 makes it unlawful for LEAs, proprietors and governors of educational establishments to discriminate against a person in a number of respects: (a) terms of admission, (b) refusal of admission, (c) 'access to any benefits, facilities or services provided by the school or college', (d) exclusion and 'subjecting him to any other detriment'. Section 18 covers any other LEA functions not covered by section 17.

This draws our attention to a whole range of possible instances of discrimination in educational provision. Since the British educational system is highly selective, since it is about classifying and grading people, about allocating resources and opportunities, there is always the possibility of racial (and class and gender) criteria influencing those choices and decisions. Streaming, exam entry, religious admissions criteria, subject choice, careers advice, discretionary grants, allocation arrangements and 'bussing' are all examples that have been quoted over the years and sometimes been the subject of community concern and pressure group activity.

The history of 'bussing' has been dealt with elsewhere,[9] and was the subject of reports commissioned by the then Race Relations Board. Now it is generally assumed no longer to be an issue. Allocation arrangements in general, however, might still be an issue if they disproportionately affected the parental choice of particular racial groups. Similarly, in a period of school amalgamations a combination of ethnic minority patterns of settlement plus decisions about school closures might put certain children at a disadvantage in terms of access to schooling, e.g. in terms of travelling time to school, participation in extracurricular activities, etc. Whether this would constitute less favourable treatment, whether it would be justifiable as, for instance, the most efficient use of resources in a situation of surplus school places are open questions. But it does indicate that legal concepts, when translated into real situations, can elucidate the social (racial) consequences of apparently neutral educational decisions. In the case of streaming, for instance, Afro-Caribbean parents sometimes report that teachers say that their child is 'doing well' yet, come exam entry time, discover that their child is entered for

CSE rather than GCE; i.e. that the child has been 'doing well' in the lower stream and 'doing well' in terms of what the teacher expects of black pupils, which may be very little. Furthermore, methods of assessment used for stream placement, if culturally biased, could be indirectly discriminatory.

But perhaps the longest standing issue in this area has been that of the suspension of black pupils from school and/or their referral to special schools and disruptive units. Afro-Caribbean parents have frequently alleged that their children are more readily suspended from mainstream education and more likely to be defined as Educationally Subnormal (ESN) than their white peers. If we dispense with any (racist) assumptions that black children are inherently more disruptive or subnormal than others, then, using the concepts of discimination in the law, our attention should be directed to looking at the practices and procedures whereby children come to be labelled as 'disruptive' or 'subnormal'. That teachers may experience, and treat, black youth as potentially troublesome or ESN, according to Sally Tomlinson, is not fanciful. In commenting on the Warnock report that preceded the 1981 Education Act on special education, she suggests that:

> The stereotypical beliefs which professional people hold about West Indian children's ability, behaviour and attitudes to education, together with an acceptance that these are somehow 'natural' racial attributes, have in the past made it likely that West Indian children met the criteria for referral to special education. The way the educational retardation of West Indian children is explained in terms of (racial) family environment and organisation and socialisation, contributed to the common sense understandings that this over referral did not really merit discussion. The assumption that black children started equal in the referral and assessment process, with no account being taken of the hostile white society, or the colonially influenced beliefs of professionals, have further 'disadvantaged' West Indian children in the process leading to ESN-M schooling. There is no reason to suppose that under the new Warnock suggested procedures, beliefs and assumptions about black children will be changed. Indeed the teachers, who hold the most stereotyped views, are to be the very people who will initiate the stages of decision making as to whether a child has 'special educational needs'... Warnock's recommendations, when applied to West Indian children, would appear either naive or politically motivated.[10]

Can Tomlinson's trenchant comments about teachers' stereotyping be extended to remedial and English as a Second Language (ESL) provision? How do teachers react to pupils for whom English is not a first language and do arrangements for ESL disadvantage certain children in terms of access to mainstream education (to 'any benefits, facilities or services')?

Speculations apart, there is at least one clear and well-documented example of discrimination[11] in education, the charging of higher fees to overseas students. This form of discrimination, however, is not unlawful in that it is covered by section 41 of the Act. This section provides that any act of discrimination is lawful if it is done in pursuance of any Law, Order in Council, Statutory Instrument or with the approval of a Minister of the Crown; apparently you or I may not discriminate, but the government can.

Finally, with reference to sections relating specifically to education in the Race Relations Act, section 71 places a duty on local authorities to 'make appropriate arrangements' with a view to securing that their various functions are carried out with due regard to the need to 'eliminate discrimination and promote equality of opportunity and good relations between persons of different racial groups'. Of all the sections of the Race Relations Act this is the one most frequently, and often exclusively, referred to by LEAs. Most of the LEA policy statements on multiracial education (of which there are now many) are presented as being in compliance with, or in recognition of, section 71 duties. Yet ironically this section of the Act is the vaguest and least enforceable. As the CRE consultative paper laments:

> This section has caused a deal of frustration. The only enforceable duty it imposes on a local authority is to determine what the 'appropriate arrangements' should be. So long as it gives the matter thought its conclusion cannot be challenged.[12]

Nonetheless, section 71 has been used by LEAs to justify a wide range of discussions and initiatives in multi-racial education. It is strange that they have not taken similar notice of other sections of the Act, but have concentrated on that section of the law described by a Parliamentary Select Committee as a 'dead letter'.[13]

EMPLOYMENT

Schools, colleges and LEAs are not only providers of services, they are also major employers, so a brief outline of the employment provisions of the Act is highly relevant to this discussion. Section 4 of the Act covers discrimination in employment with reference to recruitment, conditions, promotion, dismissal, training and any other 'benefits, facilities or services'.

The non-recognition of overseas trained teachers' qualifications by the DES is presumably covered by section 41 (referred to above), but the experiences of British born and educated black teachers is frequently described by them as one of discrimination. And this is not just in terms of initial appointment but also promotion, access to INSET, secondment and general treatment by colleagues; and it has often been alleged that black teachers are disproportionately in supply of scale 1 posts. Little systematic empirical evidence exists, however, on the employment situation of black teachers since neither the DES nor LEAs maintain ethnic records. This lack of data should be rectified, at least in part, by a CRE survey currently in progress on the position of black teachers in eight LEAs—whether this will establish any pattern of discrimination in terms of the law remains to be seen.

Several other employment-related sections of the Act are worth mentioning in relation to education. Firstly, section 32, concerning 'vicarious liability', states that an employer is held to be responsible for any act of discrimination done by one of his/her employees, whether or not it was done with the employer's knowledge or approval. In the case of LEAs, this of course applies to non-teaching as well as teaching staff. Suppose, for instance, that a school caretaker or lettings officer discriminated against community groups (e.g.

mother tongue classes) in the letting of school buildings, then the LEA could be held responsible as well for the discriminating act. However, if the employer 'took such steps as were reasonably practicable' to prevent the employee from discriminating, then the employer would not be held responsible. Whether an LEA equal opportunities or multiracial education policy would constitute 'such steps' would depend on the particular circumstances, but, in the case of the Bristol teacher quoted earlier, it is unlikely that the authority could have been held responsible for such day-to-day staffroom incidents.

Secondly, the growth of the Manpower Services Commission (MSC) and Youth Training Scheme (YTS) courses raises a number of employment/education issues where the Race Relations Act can be of guidance to those in the further education sector, particularly regarding work experience courses. Following *Daley* vs. *Allied Suppliers Ltd.*, it was realized that the protection of the Race Relations Act did not extend to the work experience element in MSC training courses. In 1983 the Secretary of State made a designation order under section 13 of the Act so as to safeguard trainees at the point of entry to, and dismissal from, work experience. Yet the law still does not cover the treatment of trainees *within* the work experience situation. However, if the work experience employer instructs or puts pressure on further education staff not to send him/her black trainees, then the employer is in breach of sections 30 and/or 31. Furthermore, if the college complies with such a request it could be in breach of section 33 in that it has aided an unlawful act. Pressure or instructions to discriminate by employers is also relevant to schools and the careers service. Careers officers and teachers may be reluctant to send black school-leavers to certain employers whom they suspect might discriminate; they should report this rather than collude with it. Finally, a general point about the Manpower Services Commission. There is some concern that black school-leavers are being shunted into those YTS courses that are least likely to lead to employment, i.e. Mode B non-employer-based schemes.

POSITIVE DISCRIMINATION

There is no concept of positive discrimination in the Race Relations Act, at least not in the American or Plowden senses of that term, and reverse discrimination, quotas and 'equality targets' would all be unlawful under existing legislation. What *does* exist in the Race Relations Act are a number of sections that allow forms of positive provision in terms of employment, training and the meeting of special needs.

Thus section 5 excludes from employment discrimination 'any employment where being of a particular racial group is a genuine occupational qualification'. This is most frequently applicable for reasons of authenticity in the catering and entertainment industries, e.g. a Chinese restaurant may advertise for a Chinese waiter. But 'genuine occupational qualification' might extend to education in circumstances where, in the words of the Act, 'the holder of the job provides persons of that racial group with personal services promoting their welfare, and those services can most effectively be provided by a person of that racial group'. Mother tongue teachers, nursery nurses, youth workers?

Section 35 allows 'any act done in affording persons of a particular racial group access to facilities or services to meet the special needs of that group in regard to their education, training or welfare, or any ancillary benefits'. At first glance, this would appear to be a very broad and inclusive formulation. However, it has been little used because of a restrictive and limited definition of 'special' as meaning peculiar or exclusive to the racial group in question. Fortunately a more generous interpretation may now be possible following the 1982 Home Office guidelines on section 11 of the Local Government Act, 1966. Here 'special' has been expanded to cover 'needs that are either different in kind from, or the same as but proportionately greater than those of, the rest of the population of the area'. Nonetheless, ideological opposition to utilizing section 35 in education may persist, given the history of 'colour blindness' on the part of teachers and a preference for subsuming 'racial disadvantage' under broader notions of disadvantages shared with other pupils. Attempts to turn the concept of 'meeting special needs' into forms of 'positive discrimination' are likely to be resisted.

Sections 37 and 38 permit (limited) forms of discriminatory training for a particular racial group by designated training bodies and employers. However, such provision is complicated by the need to show that the racial group in question were under-represented in the work force.[14] Nonetheless, section 37 has been used to develop 'access' courses to higher education designed to recruit more black teachers and it would be theoretically possible, for instance, for an LEA (as an employer under section 38) to put on training courses for black education department employees in order to equip them for more senior posts, though discrimination at the point of recruitment remains unlawful. However, it is essential to remember that the above positive sections are *permissive*, not obligatory. There is nothing in these sections of the Act that could be interpreted as an injunction or instruction; they simply allow certain types of action in particular and specific circumstances. Under current legislation 'positive discrimination' is a misnomer.

INCITEMENT TO RACIAL HATRED

Teachers sometimes wonder if the Race Relations Act can be used to deal with what they regard as the racist nature of some educational materials or with racist activities on school premises.

Section 70 of the Race Relations Act amends section 5 of the Public Order Act, 1936, and makes it an offence to publish or distribute written matter, or to use words in a public place 'which are threatening, abusive or insulting, in a case where, having regard to all the circumstances, hatred is likely to be stirred up against any racial minority'. Though the CRE receives a regular stream of complaints about school materials, it is very unlikely that the type of ethnocentrism and racial bias contained in a surprisingly large number of school texts and children's books could be construed in law as likely to stir up racial hatred.

Organized racist activities or the distribution of racist literature by political groups on school premises could be another matter. Under the Representation of the People Act, 1949, candidates in parliamentary or local elections are entitled to use school premises for meetings in the furtherance of their candidature. Since such meetings are public (and have to be for entitlement under the above Act), it is conceivable that statements made by racist or fascist candidates might fall within the meaning of incitement in the Public Order Act. However, bringing a successful case is not easy. Firstly, it is not the words as such that matter but their likelihood of stirring up racial hatred 'having regard to all the circumstances'. And secondly, prosecutions for incitement can only be brought by or with the consent of the Attorney General (not the CRE), nor do the police have powers of summary arrest. Despite these shortcomings, it is interesting to note that one LEA[15] thought the Public Order Act relevant enough to circulate all its teachers with a leaflet drawing their attention to the law, and in another instance racist literature being handed to school children has been successfully prosecuted.[16]

ENFORCEMENT

According to Lustgarten there is:

a vivid contrast between the wide-ranging scope of the law and its sophisticated definition of discrimination, and the relatively primitive and toothless devices created for the realisation of rights under it.[17]

However 'toothless' these devices might be, it is necessary to give a brief outline of them. Basically there are two legal procedures available: individual complaints and formal investigations.

1. *Complaints.* Complainants may take their cases directly to industrial tribunals (in employment cases) or county courts (in non-employment cases). Also complainants are entitled, under section 66, to seek assistance (advice, legal representation, etc.) from the CRE and about 1000 applications are received a year, of which the majority relate to employment.

This represents a very small number of potential cases given the extent of discrimination documented by social scientists and acknowledged in various government and official reports. Apart from the prospect of prolonged litigation, the reluctance of individuals to seek legal redress is probably due to fear of victimization (though complainants are specifically protected by section 2 of the Act), lack of knowledge of the law and the derisory damages awarded. Furthermore, the success rate for cases does not inspire confidence in the law. For instance, in 1982 only 30 out of 200 discrimination cases brought before industrial tribunals were successful. This high failure rate is probably due to the fact that:

> discrimination is rarely overt and the success of cases depends very much on tribunals' willingness to draw inferences. Discrimination cases of all sorts amount to a little over 25 per cent of all tribunal cases, and the infrequency of a discrimination case coming before a particular tribunal means that members' inexperience and consequent reluctance to draw inferences is...a strong factor in the unwillingness of tribunals to find discrimination proved.[18]

2. Investigations. Under section 48(1) of the Race Relations Act the CRE is empowered to conduct formal investigations in pursuance of its duties to eliminate discrimination and promote equality of opportunity (the Commission's duties are set out in section 43 of the Act). In theory, two types of investigation are envisaged. A general or strategic investigation, section 49(3), can be mounted where no allegation of discrimination has been made. A 'belief' investigation, section 49(4), takes place when a named person is alleged to have committed an unlawful discriminatory act. In practice, things are rather more complicated and, as Applebey and Ellis point out, section 49 'has proved to be one of the most problematic parts of the legislation'.[19]

Not only are there ample safeguards for the respondent to make representations objecting to the commencement of a proposed investigation, but a series of judicial decisions appear to have blunted the investigative instrument even further; namely that general investigations may no longer be possible and that 'belief' investigations require a preliminary inquiry to establish that there is sufficient evidence to constitute grounds for a 'belief'. So complicated have the legal issues become regarding the CRE's investigative powers that Lord Denning was moved to comment that:

> The machine is so cumbersome ... it is almost grinding to a halt. The Commission ... have been caught up in a spider's web spun by Parliament, from which there is little hope of their escaping.[20]

It is also worth noting that in the case of education, unlike other areas, individual complaints must first go to the DES, and non-discrimination notices can only be issued by the Secretary of State for Education, not the CRE as in any other case. It is then, perhaps, not so surprising that in the field of education the Commission has so far only published one investigation, though a second is anticipated in 1985.[21] So severe are the deficiencies of the Act's enforcement procedures according to Lustgarten that:

> a question mark hangs over the entire effort to control discrimination in Britain by legal means ... certain doctrines of substantive law, and still more the prevailing ethos among judges and other legal actors are virtually guaranteed to undermine the remedial measures required to eradicate discrimination. To put it bluntly, there is a real possibility that anti-discriminatory efforts will fall a casualty of English legal conservatism.[22]

If this outspoken assessment is accurate, then the duty of educationists to interpret the concepts of the law in an imaginative and positive way becomes *more* not less imperative; in order to implement the spirit of the law, it may be necessary to go beyond the letter of the law.

CONCLUSION

Apart from explaining the Race Relations Act in a fairly simplistic way, the above account has attempted to suggest that the law contains a number of concepts which could be fruitfully applied (albeit not always in a strictly legal sense) to educational settings; to help teachers and administrators, as Davis puts it, 'identify their professional duty'. In this respect the law also raises a more general issue concerning notions of equality and justice highly pertinent to, yet strangely ignored by, current debates in multi-cultural and anti-racist education. I refer in particular to the concept of discrimination.

In the development of American and British anti-discrimination legislation (both sex and race), it is possible to detect an evolution and expansion of the concept of discrimination. In the original British legislation of the 1960s, the law was limited to the notion of direct discrimination; by the mid 1970s. the new Sex Discrimination Act and Race Relations Act respectively incorporated the notion of indirect discrimination. As Lustgarten cogently argues, these two terms rest on distinct and conflicting ideas of racial equality. Following Mayhew, he characterizes these as the 'equal opportunity' and 'fair shares' approaches.[23]

The 'equal opportunity' (direct discrimination) approach is primarily concerned with deliberate acts done by prejudiced individuals against particular victims. It rests on an abstract, minimalist theory of equality derived from nineteenth-century individualist liberal philosophy. It is concerned with formal equality of opportunity in a competitive market place. Its result is that, according to Lustgarten:

> Each complaint of discrimination becomes a highly particularised 'case' and the social structure and power relationships which ultimately determine the situation of racial minorities remain hidden from the sight of the law.[24]

By contrast, the 'fair shares' (indirect discrimination) approach is concerned with consequences, effects and outcomes and not simply with intentional and formal treatment. As such it rests on collectivist and impersonal notions of justice and equality and is concerned with the structural exclusion of racial groups. It is concerned to look beneath the surface of formal treatment and identify the discriminatory effects of institutional practices. Though the logic of this approach would be equality of outcome in terms of the distribution of society's resources, it would be quite wrong to assume that the premise of British race relations legislation was egalitarian in any wider sense, since existing (class) patterns of inequality remain untouched. This, of course, raises important questions of the relationship between race and class inequalities in education which have yet to be confronted by those active in multicultural and anti-racist education. Nevertheless, according to McCrudden the notion of indirect discrimination attempts:

> .... to circumvent the problems of proof of intentional discrimination, to go beyond its individualised nature and to provide a basis for intervening against the present effects of past and other types of institutional discrimination. ... The potential significance of the new meaning of discrimination has ... been grossly underestimated.[25]

Whatever the enforcement limitations of the Race Relations Act, McCrudden's 'institutional discrimination', derived from the law, can be of use to educationalists. Given multicultural education's preoccupation with 'symbols' and 'representations',[26] the concepts of discrimination may redirect attention to structures and processes. Furthermore, 'institutional discrimination' is a valuable complement to the now fashionable, but loosely defined, term 'institutional racism'. Either way, the law is too important to be left to the lawyers.

NOTES AND REFERENCES

I would like to thank Paul Nicholls for his advice on a number of points of law.

1. Davis, G. How pervasive is white superiority? *Education*, **22**, 6, 1984, p. 511.
2. Menter, I. Multicultural education: Avon's calling, *Multiracial Education*, **12**, 2, 1984, p. 9.
3. Macdonald, I. *Race Relations—The New Law*, Butterworths, London, 1977, p. 10.
4. Commission for Racial Equality *The Race Relations Act—Time for a Change*, CRE, London, 1983, p. 11.
5. Carrington, B. and Wood, E. Body Talk, *Multiracial Education*, **11**, 2, 1983, p.30.
6. Interestingly, in the United States the definition of 'justifiable' is much stricter—a restrictive employment practice that disproportionately excluded minority groups would only be justifiable if it could be shown to be directly related to job performance, i.e. necessary, *Griggs* vs. *Duke Power Company*, 401 US424, 1971.
7. However, in certain circumstances a religious requirement (e.g. entrance to a Church school) could be a form of indirect discrimination.
8. Any attempt at a 'scientific' definition of racial group would, of course, be futile, since the very notion of 'race' is a social construct; 'race' is not a fact of nature but a product of historically and culturally bound perceptions. See, for instance, Miles, R. *Racism and Migrant Labour*, chapter 2, Routledge & Kegan Paul, London, 1982.
9. Kirp, D. *Doing Good by Doing Little*, University of California Press, Berkeley, 1979, and Killian, L. School bussing in Britain, *Harvard Educational Review*, **49**, 2, 1979, pp. 185–206.
10. Tomlinson, S. *Educational Subnormality*, Routledge & Kegan Paul, London, 1981, pp. 305–306.
11. If the charging of higher fees to overseas students was based on nationality, this would be direct discrimination; if on residence criteria, this would represent indirect discrimination.
12. Commission for Racial Equality, *The Race Relations Act—Time for a Change*, CRE, London, 1983, p. 40.
13. House of Commons Home Affairs Committee, *Racial Disadvantage*, Vol. 1, HMSO, London, 1981, p. XXXVI.
14. A racial group is said to be under-represented if, at any time during the previous 12 months, either there was no one of that same group doing the work in question, or there were

disproportionately few in comparison with the group's proportion in the work force of the employer, or in the population from which the employer normally recruits.

15. London Borough of Haringey, *Racist Activities in Schools*, Haringey, 1978.
16. In this particular case, the literature was being distributed *outside* the school gates; in normal circumstances a school is not a 'public place' as defined by law.
17. Lustgarten, L. *Legal Control of Racial Discrimination*, Macmillan, London, 1980.
18. Commission for Racial Equality, op. cit., note 12, p. 9.
19. Applebey, G. and Ellis, E. Formal investigations: the CRE and EOC as law enforcement agencies, *Public Law*, 1984, p. 241.
20. Denning, M.R. *CRE* vs. *Amari Plastics Ltd*, 1982, 1QB, 1194, 1203.
21. The first investigation was into LEA arrangements for secondary school allocation in Reading, but did not establish any unlawful discrimination. The second investigation is into the suspension of pupils from schools and their referral to education guidance centres in Birmingham.
22. Lustgarten, L., op. cit., note 17, p. 187.
23. Mayhew, L. *Law and Equal Opportunity*, Harvard University Press, Cambridge, Massachusetts, 1968.
24. Lustgarten, L., op. cit., note 17, p. 8.
25. McCrudden, C., Institutional discrimination, *Oxford Journal of Legal Studies*, 2, 3, 1982, pp. 345 and 367.
26. Carby, H. Schooling in Babylon, in Centre for Contemporary Cultural Studies (CCCS) Birmingham, *The Empire Strikes Back*, Hutchinson, London, 1982, and Sivanandan A. Challenging racism, *Race and Class*. Vol. XXV, no. 2, 1983.

2

Racial Inexplicitness and Education Policy

DAVID L. KIRP

THE RACIAL TINDERBOX

The changing racial composition of the British schools, and the perceived effect of that change on the character of the institutions, rendered race of policy relevance to educationists. Numbers tell part of the story. Between 1960 and 1972, the nonwhite student population—primarily composed of children of West Indian, Indian, Pakistani, African, and Asian immigrants—grew from an uncounted handful to 279,872, nearly 4 per cent of the national total. That population is concentrated in relatively few educational authorities. A majority of nonwhites attend school in the London metropolitan area, a great many of the rest in the industrial Midlands. As of 1970, half of Britain's 146 educational authorities remained essentially all white; some 24 authorities enrolled more than 7 per cent nonwhite students. In a half-dozen authorities, all in or near London, one in every five students was nonwhite.

Racial concentration does not inherently create problems. Related factors have, however, contributed to a sense of social unease. In several cities with sizeable (and ever-growing) nonwhite student populations, whites have not hesitated to voice in clearly racial terms their discomfiture with the altered composition—and, as some would say, the altered character—of their schools. Suggestions first advanced in the early 1960s that nonwhites be schooled separately are now part of the platform of the small but noisy National Front.[1] Sporadic reports of physical violence directed toward Asian students—lunch money shakedowns, after-school bashings, and the like—un-

Source: From: Kirp, David L. (1979) *Doing Good by Doing Little, Race and Schooling in Britain*, University of California Press, Berkeley.

derscore this nativist hostility. One study finds 'a depressing amount of
hostility in the attitudes of white students to their West Indian and Asian
classmates'.[2]

Racial tensions are not the only source of race-specific concern. By the
early 1970s, assessments of student achievement confirmed the popular belief
that nonwhites were not faring well in school. A national survey of teachers'
impressions of racial minority performance concluded that nonwhites,
particularly West Indians, were doing considerably worse than average.[3]
Achievement test data collected by the Inner London Education Authority
corroborated these impressions.[4] Only 8.1 per cent of nonwhite students
performed in the upper quartile; 53 per cent were in the lowest quartile in
tested English achievement. West Indian performance was somewhat worse
than that of Pakistanis and Indians, but both fell substantially below the
average: 57.9 per cent of West Indians, 44.9 per cent of Indians and
Pakistanis, performed in the lowest quartile. In mathematics, where lack of
fluency in English should have had less of a depressing effect on achievement,
racial minority performance was actually slightly worse; here again, Asian
students' achievement was marginally higher than that of West Indians. The
lowest achievement scores were reported for nonwhites attending neighbor-
hood schools more than 60 per cent nonwhite: these students' reading scores
were half a grade to a grade and a half below those of minority students
attending 90 per cent or more white schools.

The educational careers of nonwhite students seem to mirror their test
performance. Proportionately few pursue studies beyond secondary school.
At the other end of the educational spectrum, the situation is equally
unhappy: West Indians are proportionately three and four times more likely
than whites to be assigned to classes for the educationally subnormal.[5]

Racial concentration, interracial hostility, and poor minority academic
performance: taken together, these constitute the plausible elements for a
policy conflagration. The institutions directly concerned with race policy
were not unaware of the situation. The Race Relations Board (now the
Commission for Racial Equality), charged with rectifying discrimination—if
necessary through court action—has responded to a variety of complaints
alleging discrimination in education.[6] Liberal groups concerned with one or
another aspect of race relations, ranging from the government-subsidized
community relations organizations to privately funded research groups such
as the Runnymede Trust, have addressed aspects of the issue. A parliamentary Select Committee on Race Relations and Immigration undertook three
inquiries touching upon education policy between 1969 and 1977.[7] Less
tangibly but no less significantly, there is a marked and growing recognition
on the part of minority organizations that, as the West Indian Standing
Committee stated, nonwhite children are getting a 'raw deal' in the schools.

Despite these factors, race as such has had only modest impact on the
British educational policy calculus. Little attention has been paid to the

specific problem of nonwhite underachievement. Discrimination against nonwhites in school, the predicate for American judicial intervention, has until very recently been treated as irrelevant to Britain. The possibility that school authority actions—opening and closing schools, drawing attendance boundaries, and the like—'intentionally' separated nonwhite and white students has gone unexamined because to Britons it seems on its face incredible.[8] Indeed, it is intentional racial mixing that has been challenged as racially discriminatory—exactly the reverse of the American pattern.[9]

This last, however, is a development at the margin of policy. It constitutes an exception to the deliberate and sustained effort to treat inexplicitly with race. The aim of British policy has been, on the one hand, to stress the infinitely diverse needs of individual students, and, on the other, to imbed race in some broader policy context, such as educational disadvantage. In this sense, educational policy making has been consistent with policy making in other British social services, and very different from the American approach. So beside the point is race itself that, since 1972, the national government has collected no data that would permit estimation of even the number of nonwhite students. References to the shared difficulties or shared needs, if any, of that population are thus necessarily rooted in guess work.

What analysts are inclined to treat as coherent policy is often better depicted as a series of stays against confusion, *ad hoc* responses to circumstance. British reaction to student dispersal, or bussing, for example, cannot be understood without reference to such immediate pressures. But in the main, British race and schooling policy has not been reflexive; nor can it be described as nonpolicy, a lapse of governmental attention. Quite the contrary: the de-emphasis of the racial element, unwavering from almost the first days of racial conflict a decade and a half ago, has been deliberate. Inexplicitness has been the policy goal.

THE SOURCES OF RACIAL INEXPLICITNESS

Inexplicitness with respect to the racial aspects of educational policy, which characterizes the British experience, did not arise by happenstance. It is consistent with a pronounced political and bureaucratic preference for consensual, incremental decision making, a preference threatened by the confrontationist, potentially revolutionary nature of a racial orientation. It is also traceable to a deep-seated ideological commitment to universalism in social services, and a consequent allergy to group labelling for even purportedly benign governmental purposes.

These complementary phenomena have encouraged the DES to leave race alone where possible, and also to adopt policies which render nonwhites better off in so far as they help everyone, or at least everyone in need, rather than specially benefiting nonwhites. Such an approach has been presumed likely to achieve more for racial minorities in the long run, and with rather less social pain, than the alternative of a more overtly racial focus.

Consensual decision making

When confronted by demands that it undertake almost anything, the prototypical DES response is to stress its own institutional powerlessness. At one level, this departmental modesty fairly reflects the facts. While the power formally assigned to the Secretary of State for DES by the 1944 Educational Act sounds formidable—'to secure the effective utilization by local education authorities under his control and direction, of a national policy for providing a varied and comprehensive educational service in every area; [to prevent] any local education authority... [from] act[ing] or proposing to act unreasonably'—the reality is considerably less prepossessing.

The statutory provision permitting the Secretary of State to overturn 'unreasonable' local authority actions was thought to grant essentially unlimited discretion. A 1976 decision of the House of Lords, however, read this grant of power narrowly: only if no reasonable local authority could have reached a particular decision is the Secretary of State justified in intervening.[10] This court decision arose in the context of a challenge to the DES's demand that all authorities shift to comprehensive secondary schools, undoubtedly the major educational policy initiative of the past 15 years. The judicial setback to that effort, even though quickly overcome by positive legislation, doubtless diminished the department's desire further to test the scope of its broad legal mandate. The more specific powers granted by the 1944 act are, in the main, 'limited, mostly financial and negative'.[11] At least until very recently, direction giving with respect to race has not been among these specific mandates.[12]

By itself, lack of authority does not explain the DES's tendency not to intervene in a great many educational matters. The department could, after all, seek further powers by proposing new legislation; and the example of continental European systems, where substantially more authority lodges in the central educational administration, is familiar. But more power, in the formal sense, is apparently not wanted. The British educational system is conventionally described as a partnership of national government and local authorities. The complex web of interrelationships—not only among government entities but also among teachers' and headmasters' and parents' groups, research and exam-writing organizations, numerous special interest organizations, and the like—betokens a form of governance more subtle than partnership. The Permanent Secretary of DES did not exaggerate when declaring: 'Consultation is a way of life with us.'[13]

In such a 'pluralistic, incremental, unsystematic, reactive'[14] system, formal power counts for less than informal suasion. Bold initiatives are far less common than nuanced pressures on local authorities—through the inspectorate, for instance, which assesses their instructional offerings. Occasions when a policy change—such as adopting the comprehensive structure—is required, not merely recommended, are rare. In a ministry described by the Organization for Economic Co-operation and Development (OECD) as 'pragmatic, conservative and evolutionary, not theoretical, futurologic, and revolutionary',[15] few rules will be issued, except after the achievement of consensus. This is so not only because the department's formal rule-making powers are bounded, a fact that became fully evident only in 1976, but because rule making intended to alter local authority behavior is uncongenial.

In such an environment, there are few worse failings than to attempt leadership, only to discover an absence of followers. That was the fate of the 1965 DES circular recommending that authorities disperse, or bus, in order to break up concentrations of immigrant students. Many authorities, among them those with the greatest number of nonwhite students, either ignored or publicly opposed the suggestion. Circulars are supposed to have received general approval from the interested and politically significant parties before being issued; that this one hadn't was painfully evident. The denouement of the dispersal issue, a gradual DES retreat from its bussing recommendation, was not one which the department might be thought eager to repeat. It may well have promoted departmental caution with respect to race more generally.

The DES's negative response to the Select Committee recommendation that the department allocate money specifically for immigrant education programs and monitor local authority efforts was also consistent with its apparent lack of taste for directive behavior. The proposal, the DES declared, presumes:

> that local education authorities will not take initiatives to improve the education of immigrants unless there is an earmarked Department of Education and Science fund on which they can draw to meet the cost.... The Government do not believe that [this] argument is borne out by experience.[16]

Decisions concerning the wise expenditure of limited education resources, the DES added, are properly made by local authorities. 'If specific grants for particular aspects of education in which the local authorities have previously enjoyed discretion were to be introduced, the effect might be to reduce the scope of local responsibility.'

Perhaps the DES was merely disclaiming any interest in bureaucratic expansionism. Or perhaps, in the midst of the struggle over comprehensive schooling, this was not an issue over which the department wished to brook another test of its powers, recognizing the manifest lack of consensus for any course of action. Whatever the precise reason, the institutionally rooted preference for deference to local authorities effectively limited race-specific policy initiatives.

A desire within the DES for consensus concerning the substance of policies has been matched by a desire to minimize conflict in the negotiation of policies. That fact too has had a bearing on DES reluctance to address race-specific issues; the OECD summarized the department's position on the matter:

> When it comes to planning leading to policy decisions...informal methods, utilized by sensitive and fair-minded government servants, are superior to highly structured formal procedures which invite half-baked and politically sectarian battles, and encourage demagogy, confrontation, and publicity....[17]

The DES places decided limits on the consultative enterprise, and these would naturally have tended to exclude race as a topic of widespread consultation. From the department's point of view, attending to race might have been calculated to produce bile, not balm. To note just one difficulty: How would the DES determine which racial groups to consult, without arousing controversy in the process? If the education committee of the communist Indian Workers' Association was to be called upon, what about the education committee of the fascist National Front? Better, the department might well have concluded, not to make the effort at all. At any event, the documented failure to consult minority groups—even with respect to such obvious occasions for consultation as in responding to the call for native language teaching pressed by the European Economic Community—undoubtedly contributed to a lack of any substantive focus on race.

Universalism

   Structural constraints and decision-making style only partially explain DES resistance to a race-specific focus. One needs also to understand the universalist ideology on which the provision of social services in Britain has been broadly premised for the past three decades, and the tension between race specificity and universalism.
   Central to what has been termed the postwar British revolution in social welfare policy is an ideological commitment to the universal provision of social services, rather than a selective distribution on the basis of a showing of individual indigency.[18] To have to prove oneself poor or otherwise deserving before receiving schooling or medical attention is condemned on several grounds. In so far as the selective criterion forced individuals to demean themselves in order to obtain help, it imposes a stigma. Over time, that societal stigma is thought to evolve into self-stigmatization as the needy come, because of this circumstance, to think less well of themselves. 'If men are treated as a burden to others...then, in time they will behave as a burden'.[19] Selective efforts also equate need with fault, ignoring the structural elements of modern economies that render such blaming wholly unconvincing. Moreover, selectivity creates invidious differentiations with respect to the service offered—what the poor get will be worse than what is available to the better off—and so divides the society.

A universalist approach, by contrast, in which an individual's entitlement to social service has no relationship to social status, is held to foster a badly needed sense of community, discouraging traditional class and status antagonisms. 'It is not (or should be),' argued Richard Titmuss, the most passionate postwar advocate of universalism, 'an objective of social policy to build the identity of a person around some community with which he is associated.'[20] While universalism addresses itself particularly to social class-based differentiation, this generating of national community through status-blind treatment is also thought a particularly appropriate way of drawing racial minorities into the larger society.[21]

By comparison with prewar Britain, basic individual needs—in education, health care, and social security particularly—are now far more equally met. Need itself counts for more, social status for less, than before. Not that universalism by itself ever has been or could be the basis for coherent policy: it is more a slogan, the banner for an exuberantly romantic socialism, than social reality. As long as individual demands are greater than the collective willingness to share resources, some selectivity is required; for that reason, the universalist is 'driven reluctantly towards stringency in allocation'.[22] Nor do the universalists forget that certain social categories broadly deserve to benefit from 'positive discrimination'; to ignore poverty, for instance, is only to transmit inequity by producing that mythical equality of the stork and the fox. Titmuss himself is clear on this point: 'To me, the "Welfare State" has no meaning unless it is positively and constructively concerned with redistributive justice....'[23] Yet the question remains: How can the government prefer some (and which categories of 'some'?), even as it serves all?

Positive discrimination is, then, a most problematic concept for the universalist. As Richard Titmuss has framed the issue:

> The challenge that faces us is not the choice between universalist and selective social services. The real challenge resides in the question: what particular infrastructure of universalist services is needed in order to provide a framework of values and opportunity within and around which can be developed socially acceptable selective services aiming to discriminate positively, with the minimum risk of stigma, in favour of those whose needs are greatest.[24]

Selectivity is essential, but selectivity has to be both as little noticed amid the general welfare system and as psychologically undemeaning as possible. These concerns have prompted the policy suggestion that positive discrimination 'should not be confined to particular individuals and families but must help everyone in the chosen area'[25] in that way, the 'deserving' social group member does not have to identify himself as such. Similarly, in education stress has been placed on providing resources for education priority areas, rather than on aiding particular types of individuals.[26] Although these efforts do not eliminate stigma—the 'area' approach may merely transfer stigma from the class of persons to the place[27]—the desire to reduce stigma has animated such undertakings.

Positive discrimination presents another related puzzle: can it be practised in a way that does not arouse the resentment of the nonbeneficiaries? If not, the consensual framework on which universalist policy rests, the nationally shared acceptance of the 'need to diminish both the absolute fact and the psychological sense of social and economic discrimination',[22] will collapse. Without such a consensus, the policy is, in Titmuss's terms, no longer 'socially acceptable'.

To the universalist, a race-specific educational policy properly raises all of these concerns. Special attention would predictably arouse antagonisms, not private consensus, for there is little shared sense that nonwhites are more deserving than, say, the poor generally. 'Why them and not us?' remains the likely white reaction. For this reason, local authorities have often been willing to aid nonwhites only at moments when white residents were, so to speak, looking the other way. Nor is stigmatization easily avoided; aiding racial minorities might just reinforce the long-standing British impression that these groups are, after all, inferior.

Even if the policy maker overcomes these obstacles, there remains a vital further problem: the dimensions of a positive, race-specific policy are hardly clear. The Community Relations Commission could call upon the DES to produce a 'clear and unequivocal policy' concerning race;[29] it stumbled only when it had to give substance to the suggestion. There thus exists the very real possibility that any race-specific approach would be of little use to the very group it is intended to benefit. Far better, or so it may be argued, to define educational needs in terms of language or culture, tangible concerns to which no blame could attach. Better also to stress, as the DES did, the shared 'educational disadvantages associated with an impoverished environment',[30] in the expectation that the benefits flowing to that large and amorphous group would simultaneously be felt by the smaller, more visible, more vulnerable racial minority. Given such a view of the world, one helps nonwhites by *not* favoring them explicitly. The benefits to minorities from such an approach are thought to be real if invisible—or better, real because invisible. If race is officially ignored, even against the weight of the evidence, its relevance might just disappear over time.

The ideological preference for universalism, which finds more mundane expression as unhappiness with 'special treatment' or 'favoritism', has been conjoined with a style and structure of decision making resistant to definitive policy making of any sort. Arrayed against these, the bases for a race-specific policy appear, on close inspection, quite weak. In Britain, the minority population has never been able to coalesce into a community; it remains fragmented and innocent of the political arts.[31] The race relations cottage industry, functioning both inside and outside of government, has not been taken particularly seriously by the DES. Moreover, as the parliamentary Select Committee on Race Relations and Immigration noted in 1974, the two government-created agencies, the Community Relations Commission and the

Race Relations Board, have failed 'to make sufficient impact or to gain the confidence of the ethnic communities'.[32] Because the nongovernmental groups' energies have been committed to battling against increasingly restrictive immigration laws, it has been difficult, as a practical matter, for them to argue simultaneously for liberalized immigration—in part on the grounds that immigration is not problem creating—and for attending to the problems associated with race.[33] The academic community has had little of policy relevance to offer, and what it has contributed has tended to downplay the importance of race. There thus has been no effective counterforce to the racially inexplicit policies consistently pursued by the DES.

INEXPLICITNESS, RACE, AND SCHOOLING

In several related ways, the DES has pursued a policy of inexplicitness with respect to issues of race and schooling. The DES has consistently defined educational problems posed by the nonwhite presence in nonracial terms: as reflecting language difficulties or lack of cultural familiarity, or as an indistinguishable aspect of the dilemmas associated with educational disadvantage generally. Challenges to that policy—the insistence that race-specific measures be attempted, especially on behalf of West Indian schoolchildren—have been rebuffed by the DES, which has been unwilling even to maintain a count of nonwhites in British schools.

Just what is one to make of British race and schooling policy? A decade ago, Richard Titmuss chided America for not adopting a universalist approach:

> The American failure has been due to the belief that poverty was the problem and that [within the context of poverty] the advance of the poor Negro could be presented as a pro-Negro enterprise. This has not been seen as a universalist problem of inequality, social justice, exclusion.[34]

Turnabout is fair play: or so the American ambassador to the United Nations, Andrew Young, presumably thought when, flipping Titmuss's argument on its head, he criticized Britain as 'a little bit chicken' on matters of race.[35] For their part, the British, who used to discern the virtues of their own approach to race by contrasting Britain's relative tranquillity with the plagues that beset the American house, are no longer so convinced of their own rightness. A parade of critics has chided the government in general, and the DES in particular, for its inattentiveness to nonwhite concerns. The parliamentary Select Committee on Race Relations and Immigration scorned the DES for its haphazard responses to the issue; the Community Relations Commission and the privately financed Runnymede Trust have used harsher language in conveying the same point of view.

While it may be in the nature of things for organizations concerned primarily with race policy never to feel that their constituents are treated well enough, something more than interest group politics is going on here. In an open letter to the Secretary of State for the DES, Peter Walker, the Conservative MP, noted the department's 'remarkable complacency' with respect to racial issues. The Labour Party's Home Policy Committee has weighed in with an assault on 'long periods of [DES] inaction punctuated by hasty and inadequate measures' concerning race.[36]

These arguments are not new, but only now do they appear to be having some effect. The 1976 Race Relations Act specifies that discrimination with respect to education is unlawful; the predecessor act spoke only of discrimination with respect to services generally. The new act also empowers the DES to review local education authority behaviour and to consider individual claims of discrimination before these are brought to court. These provisions oblige the DES to develop some policy, at least with respect to discrimination questions, if not the broader problems of race. For another, immediately following the publication in 1977 of the Select Committee's Report on the West Indian community, the DES indicated its willingness to undertake an inquiry into the specific causes of West Indian underachievement in British schools.[37] Where research goes, demands for further governmental attention—most likely, for money on the heads of nonwhite students—are sure to follow. The result is likely to be a more direct DES involvement with race than has thus far been the case. Is this a sensible policy course?

Providing benefits for the poor without stigma constituted a vital social policy problem for postwar Britain. Adding a racial element only complicates the task. As Titmuss ruefully noted: 'Redistribution is now inextricably mixed up with the challenge of social rights as well as civil rights for "coloured" citizens.'[38] From the viewpoint of the critics, the British response has failed on two counts. It has not involved racial minorities, as communities, in the process of determining their own fate. It has also provided meagre substantive 'benefits' for the nonwhite community.

In all the discussions over the proper place of race in educational policy, nonwhite voices have seldom been heard. The government undertook to act in the best interests of a silent constituency. It acted for the racial minorities rather than with them, and in that sense was truly paternalistic. Neither universalism, the broad policy objective, nor consensualism, the preferred style, were inventions of the minority communities.

Because there was no 'nonwhite community', at least in the political sense, it may be argued that decisions had to be made on its behalf. That response is not necessarily persuasive. A study of the collapse of one civil rights group, the Committee Against Racial Discrimination, in the late 1960s, concludes:

> Given a broad definition of social rights that includes some concept of cultural diversity, the attempt by government to guarantee social rights for all citizens—regardless of race—may require more than a redistribution of social benefits; it may also require a redistribution of power, through which groups of immigrants can participate as political equals in a collectivist, pluralist political system.... The challenge to government is to share power as a means of developing the organizations or institutions for immigrants and their children.[39]

Concern about participatory values might matter less had the minority community benefited tangibly, in substantive terms, from the policy of racial inexplicitness. Inexplicitness might, in other words, be viewed not as betokening policy neglect, but rather as doing good by stealth, involving quiet good works which could not have been undertaken explicitly. If one takes spending as an empirical measure of benefit, this does not appear to have been the case.[40] In 1975–76, central government expenditure for private and secondary education (excluding special programs and school meals) totalled a bit more than 3 billion pounds. Some 12,215,000 pounds, four-tenths of 1 per cent of the education budget, were used to subsidize teachers' salaries in communities with substantial immigrant concentrations under Local Government Act. An estimated 10 per cent of the 10,022,000 pounds of Urban Programme monies spent on education went to local authority activities in which minorities were significant participants. If one makes the too generous assumption that all Local Government Act and Urban Programme monies actually were spent on nonwhites, each nonwhite child received a supplementary benefit of less than 40 pounds; in fact, since Local Government Act monies are effectively general aid for the eligible authorities, the true figure would be substantially lower.

The former DES secretary, Sir Edward Boyle (now Lord Boyle), once noted that, as concerns race and education, British policy-makers vacillate between the illusion of competence and 'talking themselves into a quite unnecessary crisis'.[41] The assault on inexplicitness falls into the latter category. If inexplicitness has not been so clearly right as its defenders have asserted, neither has it been so misguided as critics would have it. It may be best appreciated as one plausible approach to a set of immensely troubling issues.

Consider the actual policy problems that have confronted the DES. As concerns the participation issue, in the absence of sustained minority community pressure what would it have meant for government to 'share power'? Was the DES properly expected to invent a minority leadership? To put the question differently, was there really an alternative to paternalism? For the DES to undertake a 'redistribution of power' bespeaks substantive as well as processual change of most uncertain consequence. With respect to substantive matters, is it clear that a program directed particularly at minority underachievement (or minority educational *anomie*) would have done much good? Might it merely have inflated expectations without affecting educational outcomes? Would Britain's racial minorities have been better served by the British equivalent to Title I of the 1965 Elementary and Secondary Education Act, an American compensatory education program in which bookkeeping concerns—are only eligible children benefiting? —have too often driven out educational concerns—is *anyone* benefiting?

[British policy-makers] attempt a middle course between a policy of deliberate inattention, on the one hand, and an elaborate and explicitly racial undertaking, on the other. They offer no panaceas: But what alternative does? At the end of a systematic assessment of discrimination and racial disadvantage in Britain, David Smith offers a warning: 'If the children ... find that the educational system has passed them by ... then there will be the profound frustration, bitterness, and disorientation that is already seen in young West Indians....'[42] The point is well taken, and sobering for a nation just beginning to peer behind the camouflage of tolerance at its social reality. But the critical question remains: What other educational policy might Britain have pursued, with any assurance that the nation's racial dilemmas would thereby have been eased? Only the ideologue who lacks an appreciation for the ironies of social history could offer a confident reply.

NOTES AND REFERENCES

1. See Martin G. Walker, *The National Front*, London, Fontana, 1977. The National Front is more concerned about 'repatriating' the immigrants—sending them back to their country of origin—than with their treatment while in Britain.
2. Christopher Bagley and Gaiendra K. Verma, Inter-ethnic attitudes and behavior in British multi-racial schools, in Christopher Bagley and Gaiendra K. Verma (eds.), *Race and Education Across Cultures*, pp. 258, 267–269. London, Heineman, 1975.
3. H. E. R. Townsend and E. M. Brittan, *Organization in Multiracial Schools*, Slough, National Foundation for Educational Research, 1972.
4. Alan Little, The performance of children from ethnic minority backgrounds in primary schools, p. 1. *Oxford Review of Education* 117, 1975.
5. For a polemic on the subject, see Bernard Coard, *How the West Indian Child Is Made Educationally Subnormal in the British School System*, London, New Beacon, 1971.
6. See Anthony Lester and Geoffrey Bindman, *Race and Law in Great Britain*, Cambridge, Mass., Harvard University Press, 1971; Ian Macdonald, *Race Relations—the New Law*, London, Butterworths, 1978.
7. *The Problems of Coloured School Leavers*, London, HMSO, 1969; *Education*, London, HMSO, 1973; *The West Indian Community*, London, HMSO, 1977.
8. The possibility of 'intentional' segregation is not in fact incredible. In one section of London, a largely nonwhite school was said to have been kept open, in the face of declining enrolments in the area, in order to keep the minority (in this case, Bangladeshi) students in one school. Elsewhere, the proximity of largely nonwhite and all-white schools gives rise to suspicions of gerrymandering.
9. The policy of dispersing or busing only nonwhite students, as engaged in by the outer London borough of Ealing, was challenged in court by the Race Relations Board as a violation of the 1968 Race Relations Act. The 1976 Race Relations Act permits race-specific treatment to serve the 'special needs' of minorities.
10. *Secretary of State for Education and Science* vs. *Metropolitan Borough of Tameside*, [1976] 3 All ER 665.
11. Michael Locke, *Power and Politics in the School System*, p. 19. London, Routledge & Kegan Paul, 1974.
12. The Race Relations Act, 1976, section 19, declares that a local authority which discriminates in the provision of educational services is acting 'unreasonably', within the meaning of the Education Act, 1944, thus authorizing DES intervention.
13. *Tenth Report from the Expenditure Committee, Policy Making in the Department of Education and Science*, p. 110, London, HMSO, 1976.
14. Maurice Kogan, *Educational Policy Making*, p. 238. London, Allen & Unwin, 1975.
15. Organization for Economic Co-operation and Development, *Education Development Strategy of England and Wales*, p. 50. Paris, OECD, 1975. While few educational bureaucracies can be described as 'theoretical, futurological, and revolutionary', the stress on consensualism within the DES does distinguish it from other, similar bureaus.

16. Secretary of State for Education and Science, *Educational Disadvantages and the Educational Needs of Immigrants*, pp. 13–14, London, HMSO, 1974.
17. *Education Development Strategy of England and Wales*, op. cit. note 15, p. 30.
18. R. H. Tawney, *Equality*, London, Allen and Unwin, 1964, is the ideological forerunner of this movement.
19. Richard Titmuss, *Commitment to Welfare*, p. 26. London, Allen & Unwin, 1968. For a critical appraisal of Titmuss's work, see David Reisman, *Richard Titmuss: Welfare and Society*, London, Heineman, 1977.
20. Richard Titmuss, *Social Policy*, p. 38. London, Allen & Unwin, 1974.
21. Ibid.
22. Robert Pinker, *Social Theory and Social Policy*, p. 107. London, Heineman, 1971.
23. Richard Titmuss, Goals of today's welfare state, in P. Anderson and R. Blackburn (eds.), *Towards Socialism*, p. 354, London, Fontana, 1965.
24. Titmuss, op. cit. note 19, pp. 113–114.
25. Quoted in Pinker, op cit. note 81, p. 192. See also Reisman, note 19, pp. 91–98, for other redistributive techniques.
26. *Educational Priority, EPA Problems and Policies*, London, HMSO, 1972; interview with A. H. Halsey, former director of the EPA experiment, 26 June 1977.
27. A. Corbett, Priority schools, *New Society*, pp. 785–787, 30 May 1968.
28. Titmuss, op. cit., note 19, p. 182.
29. Community Relations Commission, Race and Education: a review, p. 11 (unpublished paper, 1976).
30. *Educational Disadvantage and the Educational Needs of Immigrants*, op. cit., note 6, p. 2.
31. See Ben Heineman, *The Politics of the Powerless*, London, Oxford University Press, 1972; Michael Hill and Ruth Issacharoff, *Community Action and Race Relations*, London, Oxford University Press, 1971.
32. Select Committee on Race Relations and Immigration, *The Organization of Race Relations Administration*, p. xi. London, HMSO, 1974.
33. A Fabian Society Tract scorned the 1965 White Paper, which urged restrictions on immigration, a 'major retreat from universalist values.... The restrictive policies...were bound to make racial equality harder to achieve. But they make social equality harder to achieve too.'
34. Titmuss, op. cit., note 19, p. 114.
35. *New York Times*, A5, col. 1, 7 April, 1977.
36. Home Policy Committee, Labour Party, Race and education. p. 1 (unpublished report, March 1977).
37. Interview with John Lyttle, advisor to Shirley Williams, Secretary of State for DES, 24 June 1977.
38. Titmuss, op. cit., note 19, p. 114.
39. Heineman, op. cit., note 31, p. 227.
40. John Lyttle, advisor to Shirely Williams, Secretary of State for DES, provided these figures.
41. Sir Edward Boyle, *Race Relations and Education* pp. 7–8. Liverpool, Liverpool University Press, 1970. *The West Indian Community: Observations on the Report of the Select Committee on Race Relations and Immigration*, London, HMSO, 1978. *Proposals for Replacing Section II of the Local Government Act 1966: A Consultative Document*, Home Office, 1978.
42. David Smith, *Discrimination*, p. 187. London, Political and Economic Planning, 1976.

3

Multiracial Education in Britain
from assimilation to cultural pluralism

CHRIS MULLARD

Since the early 1960s when the Commonwealth Immigrant Advisory Council recommended to the Home Secretary that special provision should be made for the education of 'immigrant' pupils, the multiracial education movement in Britain has tended to view black pupils as a *problem*.[1] They were a problem because they were black; they were a problem because many, especially those from India and Pakistan, could neither speak nor write English well enough to take an effective part in, or benefit from, school education. Numerically, they allegedly posed an administrative problem for already overcrowded inner-city schools, and a political problem which was expressed in terms of the fear that 'the whole character and ethos of the school' would be radically altered.[2] In short, their numbers, which were recently estimated to be in the order of 750,000 or roughly 8 per cent of the total school roll, represented on one level a threat and on another a challenge to our educational system, its professional organizers and political protectors.[3]

While exploratory in nature, the purpose of this chapter is to trace the educational response to the so-called 'problem' and to evaluate critically the social meanings and educational practices of multiracial education. The argument that will be unfolded here, however, will be concerned more with the social and assumptive base of multicultural education than directly with the multiracial classroom or situational conflicts arising from teaching in a multiracial school. It will be suggested that the various multiracial education models developed and employed since the early sixties have attempted to foster the cultural subordination and political neutralization of blacks; they have started to achieve the very thing many of their advocates

Source: From Tierney, J. (1982) *Race, Migration and Schooling*, Holt, Rinehart and Winston, Eastbourne, East Sussex.
Originally published in a slightly different form as "Black Kids in White Schools: Multiracial Education in Britain," *Plural Societies*, Summer 1981.

attempted to prevent—the social isolation and alienation of blacks in our society.

To begin with, however, the meaning and aims of multiracial education can be best understood if seen as the outcome of a continual process of development from intention to action, from reformulated intention to reformulated action, all stemming from a common social imperative—to maintain as far as possible the dominant structure of institutions, values, and beliefs. Although the three phases of development and meaning through which concern has travelled are to some extent interconnected and interdependent, for the purposes of our analysis here we will view them separately. They can be broadly designated the assimilationist phase, and its incumbent worldviews and model of social action which characterized thinking on race and education from the early 1950s to the *1965 White Paper*; the integrationist phase and model from 1965 to the early 1970s; and finally the present cultural pluralist phase and model which, as will be shown, is essentially a revised version of the integrationist model.

THE ASSIMILATIONIST MODEL

At the base of this model, which was dominant in the early to mid sixties and which today still influences the thinking of many educationalists, rests the belief that a nation is a unitary whole, politically and culturally indivisible. Immigrant groups, black or white, should thus be absorbed into the indigenous homogeneous culture so that they can take an informed and equal part in the creation and maintenance of our society. While a certain respect should be encouraged for other cultures and social traditions, this should be only a secondary concern. In no way should it be encouraged to the point where it could possibly undermine the social and ideological bases of the dominant white culture, or threaten the stability of what was seen as the 'host' society.[4]

For education generally the policy of cultural assimilation meant an almost obsessive attachment to the view forthrightly expressed in CIAC's Second Report; namely that:

> A national system of education must aim at producing citizens who can take their place in society properly equipped to exercise rights and perform duties the same as those of other citizens. If their parents were brought up in another culture and another tradition, children should be encouraged to respect it, but a national system cannot be expected to perpetuate the different values of immigrant groups.[5]

For teachers, as Williams describes in her study of schools in Sparkbrook, such a policy meant in practice that teachers continued to see 'their role as putting over a certain set of values (Christian), a code of behaviour (middle-class), and a set of academic and job aspirations in which white-collar jobs have higher prestige than manual, clean jobs than dirty...'.[6] Taking the point a little further, Townsend and Brittan in 1973 reported three comments on assimilation by heads of humanities departments.

The first raised the question:

> Should immigrants—from wherever they come—be encouraged to maintain the traditions and cultures of their own societies, or through an educational process, be *weaned* gradually away from this towards the adoption of the standards of the country in which about 90 per cent of them will spend the rest of their lives. The aim of the twentieth century educationalists should be to deliver mankind from the 'ghetto' mentality, be it religious or cultural...[7]

The second assumed that segregation was the only possible alternative to assimilation:

> It is assumed that immigrants wish to be absorbed into the community into which they enter; this has been indicated through experience in teaching immigrants. Features relevant to life in the British Isles are taught through the media of History, Geography and Social Studies. There are no courses in Asian History or Geography, for example, since the whole aim of the school is towards social integration. We cannot account for practices in the home which may be towards segregation.[8]

While the second teacher was quite unaware of the significant contradiction between his first and last sentences—one that perhaps helped him to justify his stance through alluding to inter-generational conflict—the third possessed few doubts over the integrity and logic of his position:

> We are after all trying to create an integrated society—and a great many of our pupils while retaining their racial and religious 'peculiarities' think of themselves as British. I think that we (the teachers) need to be made fully aware of the differences but I think in teaching we must be careful not to create divisions. Following this my History syllabus and the Humanities syllabus developing is and will remain basically British and possibly Euro-centred.[9]

Although their research is in many ways inconclusive, Townsend and Brittan show that many teachers by and large 'formed their own definition of our society and worked towards it'; definitions which ranged 'from complete assimilation through various degrees of integration (assimilation) to separate development'.[10] And from a later study conducted by Brittan it is also clear that a significant proportion of teachers perceived blacks in hostile and stereotyped terms, a threat, unless assimilated, to the smooth running of formerly all-white schools and society at large.[11] That such attitudes and indeed assimilationist conceptions of educational and societal aims often resulted in a disturbing lack of sensitivity, 'forcing' Hindu and Muslim children to eat pork and beef by adopting an English-food only school menu, coercing Muslim girls to change into PE kit and have showers, through the process of social ostracism described by Brittan and Townsend, is evidently clear from the descriptive studies that proliferate in the field.[12] But what is so often overlooked and under-analysed, as Street-Porter rightly points out, is what exactly constitutes this British society and way of life cherished by assimilationists?[13] Or to put it another way, what, apart from the unitary notion of the nation, are the other assumptions on which the assimilationists' model is based?

RG–D

From the teachers' statements quoted above, it is clear that the second assumption, which, of course, is intrinsically related to the first, is that there exist an almost definable shared value, belief system and code of behaviour into which *all* should be assimilated. This is not only, as Williams noted, interpreted to be predominantly middle class in all respects, but it is also seen to include quite centrally a stratified view of society in which pupils or adults-to-be will be placed hierarchically and ranked according to how well they have internalized middle-class values and norms.[14] That is to say, a basic tenet of assimiliationist ideology appears to reflect and dovetail with the way in which many teachers perceive the social aspects of their educational roles, such as the assessment of social as well as intellectual ability, the preparation of pupils to take up their already designated and presumed positions in the adult world of work and the social structure in general. Whether or not this, as a visible aspect of institutionalized racism, partly accounts for Smith's 1976 finding that only 31 per cent of black graduates in his sample compared with 79 per cent of white graduates managed to gain professional or management positions is debatable.[15] But, according to Smith, what is not is their command and standard of English. He concludes:

> It might be suggested that inadequate English is the explanation of the low job levels of Asian men, even after their qualification level has been taken into account but this is not so. We have seen that there is a very strong relationship between fluency in English and academic qualifications—so strong, in fact, that nearly all Asian men with degree equivalent qualifications speak English fluently. Nevertheless a substantial proportion of them (21 per cent compared with 0 per cent of white graduates) are doing manual jobs.[16]

To invert this finding slightly, a third assumption embedded in the assimilationist's model embraces the theory and rationale behind the massive 'English for Immigrants' campaign launched by the DES in 1963, taken up by the 45 or so community relations councils, and implemented almost without question by literally hundreds of primary and secondary schools designated 'multiracial'.[17] If black children could be taught English quickly and to an acceptable level then just as quickly they could be assimilated into the British educational system, and ultimately into society as a whole. Although there was then and possibly still is now a need for special and extra tuition in English, the point we are making is not one about standards or even extra-curricula activity. Hinted at by James, it is a point about social stability as expressed in the view:

> That a dose of systematic language teaching, preferably carried out in the monastic security of a special class or centre, using the seemingly efficient sub-behaviourist 'direct method' of the 1950s, would act as a lubricant; the children could be fed into the educational machine on completion of this treatment without causing it to seize up.[18]

In other words the assimilationist perspective was seen by many educationalists, politicians, and race professionals alike as one that embodied a set of beliefs about stability. The teaching of English along with a programme of cultural indoctrination and subordination, as we shall see below, would help in short to neutralize sub-cultural affinities and influences within the school. A command of the dominant group's language would not only mean blacks could 'benefit' from the 'education' provided in school, but, more significantly, it would help counter the threat an alien group apparently poses to the stability of the school system and, on leaving, to society at large.

Closely related to this viewpoint, as both a political and educational strategy for implementation and as a further base assumption of the assimilationist model, rested a notion of coercion and control. Visibly detectable in the recent much criticized government and LEA policy of dispersal, which was not officially abandoned by the former body until 1973/4, its genesis stemmed from the prevalent belief in the early 1960s that:

> The presence of a high proportion of immigrant children in one class slows down the general routine of working and hampers the progress of the whole class, especially where the immigrants do not speak or write English fluently. This is clearly in itself undesirable and unfair to all the children in the class. . .[19]

Taking up the CIAC Report's main conclusion that the dispersal of black children would be preferable, as a last resort, to *de facto* segregation, the then Minister of Education, Sir Edward Boyle, informed the House of Commons in November 1963 that:

> If possible, it is desirable on education grounds that no one school should have more than about 30 per cent of immigrants. . . . It is both politically and legally more or less impossible to compel native parents to send their children to school in an immigrant area if there are places for them in other schools.[20]

Eighteen months later the idea that white pupils would be protected educationally against the needs of black children, that they would be neither 'bussed' nor forced to change schools, was endorsed in Circular 7/65 which, in effect, officially introduced the policy of dispersal. Under a section headed 'Spreading the Children', it stated:

> It will be helpful if the parents of non-immigrant children can see that practical measures have been taken to deal with the problems in the schools, and that the progress of their own children is not being restricted by the undue preoccupation of the teaching staff with the linguistic and other difficulties of immigrant children.[21]

Thus in order to maintain standards of education in schools attended by 'large numbers of immigrant children with language difficulties' special arrangements must be made to teach them English:

> Such arrangements can more easily be made, and the integration of immigrants more easily achieved, if the proportion of immigrant children in a school is not allowed to rise too high. The Circular 7/65 suggests that about one-third of immigrant children is the maximum that is normally acceptable in a school if social strains are to be avoided and educational standards maintained. Local Education Authorities are advised to arrange for the dispersal of immigrant children over a greater number of schools in order to avoid undue concentration in any particular school.[22]

Embedded then in this racially discriminatory policy and indeed in the philosophy on which it was based lurked not only the dubious contentions that the education of white pupils would suffer in schools which possessed a large number of black pupils, that large numbers of blacks in a particular school by virtue of their being black, culturally different, would be disruptive; and that social strain allegedly caused by *them*, as blacks, would somehow inevitably lead to a general lowering of educational standards. But less difficult to fathom was the idea that assimilation could be achieved through the controlled dispersal of black pupils; that, furthermore, a measure of coercive control, national and local state direction was socially necessary to both stimulate the process of assimilation and, ultimately, to guarantee the absorption of black immigrants into white society.

All these four assumptions rely, as does the whole assimilationist model, on a fifth and in many ways a crucial belief in the cultural and racial superiority of the 'host', metropolitan society—on racism. Hidden in the recesses of rationalized thought, and built into the very structure of policies ostensibly concerned with English tuition, dispersal, and educational testing, is, as convincingly demonstrated by Coard, the imputation that black culture is inferior, that black values and beliefs are of secondary importance, even whimsical, when considered against those held by dominant white groups.[23] To assimilate, for blacks, is to discard voluntarily or to be forced to discard all that culturally defines their existence, their identity as West Indians, Asians, or Africans. To assimilate, for whites, means to stay the same. That such a model's social anchorage and, moreover, political thrust depends upon an ethnocentric conception of our society, an almost rigid belief in the superior value of western culture and institutions, is also evident in headteachers' statements on the subject of multiracial education. Simply:

> Continuous discussion of racial differences in culture and tradition serves only to perpetuate them. I do not consider it the responsibility of an English state school to cater for the development of cultures and customs of a foreign nature. I believe our duty is to prepare children for citizenship in a free, Christian, democratic society according to British standards and customs...[24]

The integrationist model

Compared with the model out of which it evolved, the integrationist perspective is less crude. Many politicians, including the former Home Secretary, Roy Jenkins, and possibly even more teachers by the mid 1960s, had already started to reject the inherently racist nature of the assumptions underpinning the assimilationist model. The former, for instance, urged that what was required was 'not a flattening process of assimilation but equal opportunity, accompanied by cultural diversity, in an atmosphere of mutual tolerance'.[25] In other words, and on the surface at least, the idea of cultural superiority, which had sustained the early and continuing influence of those who advocated assimilation, should be replaced by the intrinsically more liberal and humanitarian concept of cultural tolerance. Further, and an important departure from earlier views, this definition of integration accepted that equal opportunities did not exist, that racist views and practices, institutionalized or otherwise, had in fact inhibited the development of equal opportunity structures and the creation of a racially harmonious and equal society. It also attempted to shift the emphasis of thought and policy away from social and cultural imperatives, and towards political integration. From a position of expected equality which in turn would be achieved through providing equal educational, social, and economic opportunities, black groups, or so it seemed, would be able to renegotiate their position in society with the various dominant power groups. Although this seemed eminently preferable to the assimilationists' overt injunction 'to integrate on our terms', (or else), the gap, as Street-Porter stresses, between the idealism expressed by Jenkins and the practical implementation of integrationist policies was acute and clearly demonstrated in educational practice.[26]

She opens:

> The late sixties saw the start of several small policies which reflected partly the views of the Jenkins statement and also the assimilationist hangover.... There was a mushrooming of courses and conferences to inform teachers about the homeland of such British-born children and there was an increasing number of advisory posts created to deal with the 'problems' of 'immigrant' education.... Dispersal was officially abandoned, concern expressed about West Indian children in ESN schools, and an increasing amount of money was being spent on the special needs of such children.[27]

By way of an overall explanation, she concludes:

> Cultural integration seems to have been accepted merely as a modest tokenism, an acceptance of that which is quaint in a minority culture but a worried rejection of those cultural aspects that seem not just alien but threateningly so. In other words minority groups in practice are allowed complete freedom to define their own cultural identity only in so far as this does not conflict with that of the white indigenous community.[28]

While this might appear to represent a plausible analysis of why integrationist educational policies have not worked in practice, it fails, unfortunately, to come to grips with the actual assumptions on which the integrationist model is based.

The Select Committee had this to say in response to the Committee on Black Studies memorandum:

> The demand for black studies has arisen because the content of education in Britain is seen as Anglo-centric and biased against black people. We can understand this. But we doubt whether black studies in the narrow sense would make a contribution to wider education and better race relations, and we are not attracted by the idea of black teachers teaching black pupils in separate classes or establishments.... We come down firmly on the side of unity through diversity.[29]

Although the phrase 'unity through (cultural) diversity' appears to be a paraphrasing of the explicit social ends of Jenkins's original conception of an integrationist policy, it differs little from the assimilationist's belief in a politically and culturally indivisible society. Where it differs is only in a matter of degree. Within this perspective, political diversity is discouraged in favour of political integration; cultural diversity is tolerable so long as it neither impedes progress to political integration nor explicitly challenges the cultural assumptions of our Anglo-centric society. That is to say the political imperative of assimilation in this model is no longer, as construed in the early sixties, dependent upon complete cultural subjugation: the means to the ends have slightly changed, but the ends remain the same. But even on this level of analysis it is still questionable whether or not cultural diversity is openly promoted. From the Select Committee's statement above, which was greeted with the full approval of the government, it is, of course, clear that blacks should 'not be expected to get rid of all their own customs, history and culture'; but by the same token it is also clear that 'those who come here to settle must, to some extent, accept the ways of the country'.[30] In other words, there exists an expectation that they will in fact 'get rid' of most of their customs, history, and culture. Indeed this covert end will be assisted by 'the educational process (which) influences and helps to shape (society)'.[31] Thus it would seem from this standpoint that toleration should be considered as a short-term social objective; an awareness and appreciation that the integration-assimilation goal can only be achieved harmoniously if blacks are conditionally allowed to maintain aspects of their culture in order to provide the sense of social security, independence, and possible confidence to integrate or assimilate at a later stage, after contact with and involvement in 'the educational process'.

The assumptions, then, of cultural superiority, social stability, and shared values and beliefs still figure prominently in this second model. Though reformulated in terms of conditional cultural diversity, the first manifests itself often in the emphasis placed on integration into *our* society, *our* way of life, which in turn undervalues, even negatively values, other cultural traditions and ways. In the school, as described to some extent by Jeffcoate and to a greater extent by Searle, it takes on an added dimension.[32] *Our* society and *our* way of life are firstly juxtaposed and secondly subtly inculcated through the adoption of a liberal ideology which promotes and stimulates classroom discussion on multiracial issues within the framework of dominant white British norms, values and beliefs. Or, to put it another way: other cultures, other ways of life whether introduced as part of the formal or informal curriculum are seen and often openly evaluated against not their own value and belief patterns but, instead, those of the school and the wider British society. Through such a process a deceptive pressure to conform is inevitably exerted; one that is channelled obliquely through the posture of liberal, multiracial education.

In fact, ultimate conformity and eventual cultural absorption become, as the assimilationist model demonstrates, preconditions of a stable and racially harmonious society. Stability as both an assumed continuing aim and present social condition likewise is based on the further assumption that there exist values and beliefs to which we *all* subscribe. All the integrationist model affords, as possibly distinct from its predecessor, is that, while immutable, these dominant values and beliefs can in effect be reinforced through following a policy of mutual tolerance and reserved respect for other cultural values and beliefs. For what matters is not total but selective value orientation and acceptance. In short, political and economic values and beliefs, those on which our society and its major institutions are based, need to be separated from the rest—religious beliefs, cultural customs, and so on. And, as the most important values and beliefs in the sense of their determining the substructural base of our society, they become the ones that must be protected at all costs and to which black pupils and adults must be persuaded to subscribe. By allowing limited diversity in respect of religious beliefs, customs, dress and even language, it is assumed within the framework of the model that blacks will be more likely to accept than reject outright those which actually shape our society.

Seen from this position, the notion of equal opportunity which occupied a central place in Jenkins's definition in essence means social control. Firstly, on a theoretical level equal opportunity for all can only exist in a society where there prevails, among other things, a general acceptance of the dominant values and beliefs. Where this does not exist, equal opportunity is dependent upon the degree of mutual tolerance to be found. But given the necessity in the first place of relying on mutual tolerance—that racism exists—it is highly likely that the degree of equal opportunity to be attained at any one time by any one group will correlate quite closely with that group's orientation towards a society's dominant value and belief system. If it rejects this system, equal opportunities of access to key positions in the power structure where social or political change can be effected will be denied; if it accepts, equal opportunity of access will possibly be granted with the understanding that the existing system of beliefs will be upheld. In other words, given the racial dimension of the structural inequality that exists in our society, equal opportunity in practice means equal opportunity only for persons whose ideas and values conform to those of the dominant white middle-class culture.

On an educational and more practical level, the provision of equal opportunities is already defined in terms of the objectives of education in British schools. For black pupils, as in many cases for white working-class children, this means the rapid development of conceptual tools, language and arithmetical skills, white middle-class values, and so on, in order to achieve academically—pass GCE examinations with the view to entering higher education. Equal opportunity tends to be interpreted in the school setting as the provision of services, facilities, resources and so on to all in order for all to have an 'equal' chance of achieving the explicitly middle-class social and educational objectives revered by the school. Those who desire social and academic achievement need foremost to conform, to accept, if only passively, the school ethos before they can usefully gain from the supposed equal opportunities provided. To integrate in this sense is to suppress the cultural symbols of one's social existence; to submit to a form of control that denies that very existence. Or, as Gus John has put it:

To wish to integrate with that which alienates and destroys you, rendering you less than a person, is madness. To accept the challenge to join it and change it from within, when it refuses to accept that you are there in your fullness and refuses to acknowledge the results of interaction between you and it, is double madness.[33]

CULTURAL PLURALISM

If the integrationist model is in fact a more sophisticated and liberal variant of the assimilationist model, then that which is constructed around the concept of cultural pluralism is in effect a more refined version of both. In many ways it is not a separate model at all; it really expands the idea of cultural diversity and establishes the existence of this idea as a central observable feature of the social structure. Certainly, in contrast to the assimilationist's view of our society as being politically and culturally homogeneous, its advocates maintain that our society consists of different groups which are culturally distinctive and separate. Therefore with a plural society there exists a positive commitment to difference and to the preservation of group culture, traditions and history. The only thing that is acknowledged as binding on all groups is the political authority of the state. Whether or not Britain is a plural society in this somewhat simplistic sense or indeed whether it exhibits any of the defining characteristics outlined by Van den Berghe is not as important a question to resolve in the context of our argument here as is the question of its relevance *vis à vis* multiracial education.[34]

On this count it appears to take the liberal idealism of the mid sixties and remould it into an operational philosophy for educational innovation and policy action. For a start cultural pluralism can mean all things to all people. For some it can mean the pursuing of a policy of total cultural segregation which in turn could lead to demands for political segregation; for another group it could mean a policy of revised integration based upon a more equitable distribution of power; and yet again for others it could be used to justify and encompass more educational development, curricular expansion and educational sensitivity.[35] Given this problem with the concept and the way it is beginning to be employed in Britain—as a revised policy of integration—it is perhaps more useful at the moment to see it not as a distinct model but as a more liberal and possibly progressive version of the integrationist model.

Although some might argue that this is a neat way of dismissing it altogether, it does, however, provide us with the opportunity, firstly, to address briefly a common underlying assumption of the two main models; and, secondly, tentatively to bring our thoughts together on the meaning of multiracial education. With respect to the first issue, one of the main problems associated with the pluralist perspective in general and that of cultural pluralism as a multiracial education model in particular, arises from the way in which it views the distribution of power in our society. In theory at least, it sees power as a residual commodity possessed by the culturally different groups that constitute a plural society. That is, simply, all groups possess power; all groups possess roughly equal amounts of power; or, if not exactly equal amounts, all groups acquire enough power to ensure the maintenance of a high degree of cultural sovereignty and distinctiveness; and all groups are able equally to assert pressure on the political state and negotiate with its agencies to see that a certain amount of cultural equilibrium is maintained. Leaving aside the crucially problematic question of the actual socio-cultural composition of the state and the even more difficult question of the nature of state power *vis à vis* that held by constituent cultural groups, the problems implicit in this perspective are still fairly obvious. Equal distribution of power will not theoretically only depend upon group size, the economic base of each group, history, the organizing ability of each group, and a host of other variables, but more significantly in a dualistic international and interlocked economy based on two competing political and economic ideologies, it will depend upon at least three other factors:

1. The precise relationship that the plural state maintains with the international economy.
2. The relationship the plural state builds with class- and ethnic-based constituent groups.
3. The relationships that exist between the constituent groups themselves.

In the context of Britain it is empirically difficult to establish that we live in a plural society in most senses of the concept. Neither West Indians, Pakistanis, Indians, nor Africans, nor blacks as a whole, possess anything like the same amounts of power as the white dominant 'British' group. So even if we were to take cultural pluralism seriously as a multiracial education model separate from that of integration, it is patently clear that black groups in a white society, black pupils in white schools, could not develop their cultural traditions without the unconditional permission, approval and encourage-ment of white society as a whole and of white dominant power groups in particular. What this then suggests is that the power assumption located at the base of the cultural pluralism model as interpreted by its mainly white British advocates—as a culturally defined form of integration—and at the base of the other two models of assimilation and integration is to all intents and purposes identical.

One headteacher got very close to the point when she asked rhetorically:

Is (Britain) a society into which immigrants are gradually absorbed into English culture? Is it a society in which the best is taken from, say, West Indian, Asian and English culture to form a basis for a new culture? Is it a society in which the English culture must adapt itself to new and increasingly powerful voices of the different cultures? Are immigrant cultural forces sufficiently powerful to encourage the indigenous population to change its cultural heritage? Will a 'ghetto' situation contain immigrant cultures and cause the indigenous population to ignore and disregard immigrants, causing a multiracial society to remain really a racial one (with the same power structure)?[36]

The point is, of course, that all the models assume various degrees of cultural change on the part of black groups in school and society without any corresponding change on the part of white groups in school and society. Power is held by white groups in society; white groups and schools can insist that black groups and pupils assimilate or integrate. Real power in a capitalist and ... a racist society is indivisible. Although disguised and dressed up with platitudes or good intentions, the three multiracial education models are in fact power models. They are power models constructed by dominant white groups for the protection of the power of white groups, for the continuation of our society as it is basically perceived by those groups.

CONCLUSION

Multiracial education in Britain, then, has above all meant the assimilating or integrating of alien black groups, without disruption, into a society dedicated to the preservation of social inequality and a seemingly unchanging and cherished stock of central values, beliefs and institutions. As interpreted and practised by many, multiracial education has appeared to become an instrument of control and stability rather than one of change, of the subordination rather than the freedom of blacks in schools and or society as a whole. In the context of schools and against a wider societal background of institutionalized racism, multiracial education programmes, from the assimilationist's view on English teaching to the integrationist's stance on multicultural and black studies, have in fact integrally contributed to the increased alienation of black youth. To be told, however politely and cleverly, that your culture and history count for nothing is to invoke responses ranging from low self-esteem and lack of confidence, as Verma and Bagley et al have convincingly shown, to political opposition and resistance. To be told that your culture and history count for something only within the pedagogic boundaries of the school curriculum and not outside the school gates in the white dominated world of work and politics is to foster the response of a 'blacks only for the black studies class'. To be goaded to integrate politically and then in practice to take up your place at the bottom of society with as much of your culture intact as is permitted is, to extend Gus John's conclusion, a madness that not even a mad and subordinated black can any longer contemplate.[37] Simply, what multiracial education, as viewed in British schools, is teaching black pupils is that they will always remain second-class citizens; and, ironically, that in order to survive or exist as blacks it is necessary to resist racist authority within and outside school.

Without a radical reappraisal of multiracial education theory and practice, our society's materialist and racist culture will continue to be transmitted by all schools: without a radical reconstruction of our society as a whole and of the meaning and practice of multiracial education in particular, we shall for some time to come continue to talk about black kids in white schools, rather than merely children in schools.

NOTES AND REFERENCES

1. See *Second Report by the Commonwealth Immigrants Advisory Council* (Cmnd 2266), London, HMSO, 1964.
2. Ibid., para. 25.
3. Although from 1966 to 1973 the DES made some attempt to collect statistics through the instrument of Form 7 (1), these proved to be inaccurate as children of mixed (black) immigrant and black/white non-immigrant parentage were excluded; a ten-year rule also excluded those black children who had resided in Britain longer than this arbitrary period; and finally it also excluded the children of blacks who were themselves born in Britain. For an official discussion on the reliability of DES statistics consult Chapter 9 of the Select Committee on Race Relations and Immigration's *Report on Education*, Vol. 1, London, HMSO, 1964. Also see Street-Porter, R., *Race, Children and Cities*, pp. 63–69, Milton Keynes, The Open University Press, 1978.
4. The concept of the 'host' society as part of the 'stranger' hypothesis in race relations illustrates not only the kind of attitude that prevailed during the early 1960s but also the kind of approach developed in the study of race relations at that time.
5. *Second Report by the Commonwealth Immigrants Advisory Council*, op. cit., para. 10.
6. See Jennifer Williams, chapter 10 in Rex, J. and Moore. R., *Race, Community and Conflict: A Study of Sparkbrook*, Oxford, Oxford University Press, 1967.
7. Quoted in Townsend, H. E. R. and Brittan, E. M., *Multiracial Education: Need and Innovation*, p. 31, Schools Council Working Paper 50, London, Evans/Methuen Educational, 1973.
8. Ibid.
9. Ibid.
10. Ibid., p. 83.
11. Brittan, E. M., Multiracial education 11: teacher opinion on aspects of school life, *Educational Research*, **18**, 82–191, 1976.
12. Townsend, H. E. R. and Brittan, E. M., op. cit.
13. Street-Porter, R., op. cit., p. 77.
14. Williams, J., op. cit.
15. Smith, D.J., *Racial Disadvantage in Britain*, London, Penguin, 1977.
16. Ibid., pp. 76–77.
17. See *English for Immigrants*, Ministry of Education pamphlet, No. 43, London, HMSO, 1963.
18. See James, A., Why language matters, *Multiracial School*, Summer, 1977.
19. *Second Report by the Commonwealth Immigrants Advisory Council*, op. cit., para. 25.
20. See *Hansard*. Vol. 685, cols 433–444, 27 November 1963.
21. *The Education of Immigrants*, Department of Education and Science Circular 7/65. London, June 1965. This circular was sent to local education authorities and certain other bodies concerned with race relations and education.
22. *Immigration from the Commonwealth*. (Cmnd 2739), London, HMSO, 1961, paras. 41–42.
23. Coard, B., *How the West Indian Child is made Educationally Sub-normal in the British School System: The Scandal of the Black Child in Schools in Britain*, London, New Beacon Books, 1971.
24. Townsend, H. E. R. and Brittan, E. M., op. cit., p. 13.
25. Rt. Hon. Roy Jenkins, *Address given by the Home Secretary to a meeting of Voluntary Liaison Committees*, London, NCCI, 1966.
26. Street-Porter, R., op. cit., pp. 80–81.
27. Ibid.
28. Ibid.

52 *Chris Mullard*

29. Select Committee *Report on Education*, op. cit., paras. 102, 103 and 104, 1973.
30. For governmental approval see in particular, *Educational Disadvantage and the Educational Needs of Immigrants: Observations on the Report on Education of the Select Committee on Race Relations and Immigration* (Cmnd 5720), London, HMSO, 1974.
31. Select Committee *Report on Education*, op. cit., para. 104, 1973.
32. See Searle, C., *The World in a Classroom* and Jeffcoate, R., *Positive Image: Towards a Multiracial Curriculum*. Both are published by Writers and Readers Publishing Co-operative/Chameleon Books, London, 1978, 1979.
33. Quoted in British Council of Churches, *The New Black Presence in Britain: A Christian Security*, London, BBC Publications, 1976.
34. For a full list of the defining features of a plural society see Van den Berghe. P., *Race and Racism: A Comparative Perspective*, p. 35, London, John Wiley and Sons, 1967.
35. As Street-Porter, R., op. cit., notes, the concept, certainly in America, has become a catch-all for a whole number of policies, ranging from compensatory education to affirmative action and women's educational equality; it has become overworked and empty.
36. Townsend, H. E. R. and Brittan, E. M., op. cit., pp. 16–17.
37. Gus John in the British Council of Churches, op. cit.

4

Anti-racism as an Educational Ideology

ROBERT JEFFCOATE

THE EMERGENCE OF ANTI-RACISM

Anti-racism as a self-conscious educational ideology first emerged in the 1970s. In the early years of the decade an organization called Teachers Against Racism flourished briefly; it was later followed by others such as Teachers Against the Nazis and All London Teachers Against Racism and Facism. Anti-racism marked itself off from the liberal tradition of teaching about race relations and from the publicly advocated (but little implemented) integrationist policy of infusing the curriculum with cultural diversity. These were held to be all very well in their own way but inadequate for the pressing task of eradicating racism from the education system and combating negative influences on children in the wider society. In the 1980s anti-racism has made major political advances, recently capturing ILEA, other Labour-controlled local authorities and the influential National Association for Multiracial Education, previously a bastion of multiculturalism.

A number of factors can be detected behind the origin and growth of anti-racism in the 1970s. First, there was the accumulating evidence of underachievement among West Indians. Second, there was David Milner's replication of American research into racial identification and preference on British 5–8-year-olds in the late 1960s. Originally reported in *New Society* in 1971, his findings demonstrated the early onset of racial, and indeed racist, attitudes, with a disquietingly high proportion of West Indian and South Asian children also betraying symptoms of self-rejection (Milner, 1975). Ten years later Alfred Davey and colleagues repeated the experiment, using

Source: Jeffcoate, R. (1984) *Ethnic Minorities and Education,* Harper and Row, London.

different tests on a slightly older age-range (7–11-year-olds), and found that although self-rejection had considerably diminished, the level of stereotyping and ethnocentricism displayed by whites, West Indians and South Asians had not (Davey and Norburn, 1980; Davey and Mullin, 1982).

By this time attention had rather shifted from the embryonic racism of infant and junior schoolchildren to the virulent racialism of white, male, working-class adolescents. This provided the third main reason for the growth of the anti-racist ideology in education. White adolescent racialism was popularly associated with the recrudescence of neo-Facist groups such as the National Front, whose ranks were swelled by dissident Tories after the Conservative government's decision to admit the Ugandan Asians expelled by Idi Amin in 1972. No doubt the far Right, with its overtones of anti-establishment militarism, did make successful appeals to disaffected youth in the recruiting campaigns launched outside football grounds and at rock concerts. But 'Paki bashing' antedated the rise of the National Front and continued after the National Front and the other extremist parties of the far Right had reverted to their customary fissiparous insignificance, following the Conservative electoral victory in 1979 and Mrs Thatcher's promises of even tighter immigration controls. Evidence on the prevalence of these three phenomena—black underachievement, the incipient racism of young children and the full-blown racialism of adolescents (whether associated with the fleeting resurgence of neo-Facism or not)—has figured prominently in the anti-racist argument that what ILEA has called the 'central and pervasive influence of racism' demands a more forthright, purposeful and unremitting response than has so far been attempted.

THE MEANING OF RACISM IN THE CONTEXT OF EDUCATION

One of the problems anti-racists have in sounding convincing is that racism is used in education, as elsewhere, to cover a multitude of sins. The charge has been levelled at individual teachers and pupils, at schools as institutions and at the entire education system. These different uses need to be identified and distinguished from one another. First of all there is racism in the classical sense of a set of beliefs, largely of nineteenth-century origin, about the categorization, characterization and evaluation of human beings on the basis of their physical appearance ('scientific' racism). Second, there are the unflattering or hostile prejudices and stereotypes an individual may entertain about groups to which he or she does not belong ('popular' racism). Third, there are acts of discrimination, intimidation and violence, which some commentators prefer to describe as racialism rather than racism because they are seen as 'behaviour' rather than 'opinions' or 'attitudes'.

Finally, there is the vexed question of 'institutional' racism. I have [several] reservations about this addition to the vocabulary of race relations. Its shortcomings as a tool of analysis in the field of education are only too apparent. Whereas it is relatively clear how 'scientific' and 'popular' racism might manifest themselves in schools—in the attitudes and behaviour of teachers and pupils, in the curriculum and other aspects of school policy—what institutional racism refers to remains as obscure as in other spheres. ILEA's *Policy for Equality* defines it vaguely as a 'web of discriminatory policies, practices and procedures' whose consequence is that 'black people have poorer jobs, health, housing, education and life chances than do the white majority and less influence on the political and economic decisions which affect their lives'. The trouble with this definition is that it is based on a generalized picture of black people's position in society which the evidence has shown to be decidedly suspect. Matters have been further obscured in some quarters by the tendency to use 'institutional' racism to refer to patterns of inequality in outcome rather than, or in addition to, the policies, practices and procedures that are alleged to produce them. A good example would be the degree of black underachievement at 16+ revealed by the survey of school leavers in six LEAs undertaken by the DES for the Rampton Committee in 1978-1979. For some this underachievement is *per se* an indication of institutional racism irrespective of what might have caused it. However, it may (just possibly) be wholly unrelated to 'scientific' and 'popular' racism; or (more probably) racism in these senses may be only one factor in its complex aetiology. Institutional racism has also been applied to curriculum or organizational policy which is inappropriate to a multi-ethnic society. Again, it has to be queried whether this is a useful or valid characterization. Syllabuses in literature, geography and history which limit their choice of content to the British or European are more likely to be reflections of parochialism, teacher ignorance or sheer curriculum inertia, than of anything that could fairly be construed as racism. Similarly, failure to make concessions to ethnic minorities in such areas as school uniform or dress could be motivated as much by a wish not to be seen to favour them, as by antagonism towards them or any belief in the inferiority of their cultures.

ANTI-RACISM AS OBFUSCATION

Preoccupation with racism to the exclusion of all else, and with outcomes and effects rather than intentions or causation, goes some way to explaining why anti-racists have so frequently misidentified the nature of the problem to be addressed and been found fighting the wrong battle. Take, for example, one frequently cited instance of institutional racism—the congregation of black pupils in bottom streams or sets. Anti-racists are likely to argue not only that this is racist *per se*, but that it should be replaced by an arrangement which guarantees proportional representation. In fact the over-representation of black pupils in bottom streams or sets is not necessarily a manifestation of racism. No one *knows* why it occurs. The explanation is probably multifactoral and could well include factors falling outside the senses of racism defined earlier. Nor is such over-representation necessarily a manifestation of racial inequality. Working-class pupils have long been shown to 'percolate downwards' through streaming and setting systems. As most black pupils are working class, their position could simply be a more visible representation of this long-standing tendency.

The impression conveyed by the anti-racist argument is that all would be well if black pupils were distributed evenly across forms and sets. Given willingness on the part of the authorities, this outcome could no doubt be readily secured, but only at the expense of undermining the basis of streaming and setting which is supposed to be some kind of objective assessment of ability or aptitude. Moreover it would leave untouched the position of working-class pupils who were not black, and would mean that other children would have to be relegated to make room for the black pupils promoted. In other words the complexion or identity of those suffering the indignity of bottom streams or sets would be changed but the numbers would not. The problem is not that more black children are to be found there than one would expect from their proportion in the overall pupil population, but that any child of whatever colour or ethnic background should be exposed to such public humiliation and to the risk of depressed academic performance that is widely believed to be associated with it.

Similarly, anti-racists have been known to complain that voluntary schools situated in multi-ethnic neighbourhoods too often have fewer pupils from the ethnic minorities than would have been expected had a strict catchment area policy of school allocation been in operation; they have appeared to imply that under-representation is the extent of the problem to be rectified. Sometimes under-representation is certainly at least partly the result of church complicity in the racism of white parents anxious to reduce the incidence of contacts between their children and black people. However, it could also simply be a reflection of admissions policy favouring the faithful. Increasing the proportion of ethnic minority children attending voluntary schools could only come about as a consequence of a reversal of admissions policy (since so many of them are neither Christians nor Jews), which would no doubt somewhat affect the schools' role as institutions to preserve the faith. Yet, even were this to happen, the dual system would remain intact, arbitrarily dividing the nation's young. As in the case of streaming and setting, the problem is not so much the position occupied by pupils from the ethnic minorities, as the invidiousness of the system which their presence has served to highlight.

ANTI-RACISM AS ILLIBERALISM

The main reservations to be expressed about anti-racism concern recent initiatives by a few local authorities and schools which appear to threaten the autonomy of teachers and pupils and to evoke the spectres of indoctrination and totalitarianism. The most blatant example involves the London Borough of Brent. In 1983 its Labour-controlled council announced that, in the event of not enough teachers volunteering for 'racism awareness' courses, it would consider making attendance compulsory. Furthermore, willingness to attend would in future be made a condition of all new appointments to the borough's staff. This stipulation represents a gross infringement of teachers' rights. Traditionally, teachers have attended those in-service courses they thought would benefit their professional development, which is not to say that headteachers or advisers have not drawn their attention to particular courses and encouraged them to attend. But to make a course mandatory, or to make a new appointment conditional on attendance, is quite simply not compatible with education in a democracy—in a society where 'the individual has, in the last resort, the freedom to choose'. Nor for that matter, in this instance, is the course itself. Indeed it is peculiarly apt that courses in 'racism awareness training' should be made obligatory for they do not appear to attach any great importance to individuals thinking for themselves; and it is hard to imagine many self-respecting teachers attending courses bearing such a sinister title of their own accord.

Illiberalism is also a feature of several of the recently promulgated anti-racist guidelines and policy documents. But what is more striking is that they should also have found it necessary to state that certain forms of behaviour which have always been regarded as unacceptable and intolerable should be outlawed and punished. I have not worked in a school in which personal abuse, insulting graffiti, bullying and physical assaults were held to be anything other than serious disciplinary offences. Yet the NUT, ILEA and a number of schools have all been moved to state publicly that racialist behaviour of these kinds should be proscribed and the perpetrators chastised. I am puzzled by their motivation, for such an unwarranted intervention could well be taken to imply that racialist bullying is more reprehensible than bullying which is not racialist—surely an untenable position.

For some reason anti-racists appear to lose faith in normal democratic practice when it comes to engaging with racist opinions and beliefs. For example, several local authority and school anti-racist policies state that racist literature should be confiscated. One quotes the following extracts from a National Front leaflet found in school:

> Unfortunately, East End discos are very much multi-racial. White youths entering a discotheque in the East End might be approached by a gang of blacks who ask for some money, if the white refuses he would very probably be 'done over'.... We in the Young National Front think it's time that discos in East London and the whole of Great Britain

were designed for us. They should not be designed especially for black invaders.... The
YNF will welcome all young patriots to one of our 'ALL WHITE' discos.
The National Front wants Britain to remain a white country and for this reason it opposes
all coloured immigration to Britain. Furthermore, the National Front wants to send all
coloured people back home, to their own countries, by the most humane means possible.

(Quoted in NUT, 1983, p. 17)

The justification given for confiscation in this instance is that such literature
is like pornography—'directly offensive and degrading to many of our
pupils'. In fact the extracts quoted are decidedly *unlike* pornography. The
closest approximation to racialist abuse is the phrase 'black invaders'.
Essentially they amount to an expression of opinion, here on the desirability
of all-white youth clubs and an all-white Britain. In other words, they are an
example of the type of 'racialist propaganda' that successive governments
have consistently refused to include under the offence of incitement to racial
hatred. 'False and evil publications of this kind,' argued the 1975 Home
Office White Paper *Racial Discrimination*, 'may well be more effectively
defeated by public education and debate.... Due regard must also ... be paid
to allowing the free expression of opinion.'

Five years later a Green Paper amplified on the threat to democracy posed
by proscription:

> It would make no allowance for genuine discussion and debate or for academic consideration
> of such proposals. To single out political proposals for proscription by law regardless of how
> they are expressed, and in what circumstances, and of the possible consequences would be a
> new departure. In the Government's view such a departure would be totally inconsistent with
> a democratic society in which—provided the manner of expression, and the circumstances, do
> not provoke unacceptable consequences—political proposals, however odious and undesira-
> ble, can be freely advocated (Home Office, 1980, para. 112).

The critical point is that pupils should feel free to express their opinions in
the classroom, no matter what their political or ideological content may be,
learning at the same time (one hopes) to test them out against publicly
accredited criteria of truth and rationality and to observe the rules of
democratic procedure. It would, of course, be naive not to recognize that,
where the content is racist, particularly fraught classroom moments may
arise. Stenhouse and colleagues (1982) acknowledged that there was likely to
be something especially sensitive about race as a controversial issue; and their
classroom research shows their apprehension to have been well founded. But
this is an argument not for proscription or evasion but for developing the skill
and confidence to cope.

Another area of anti-racist activity where illiberalism has been prominent
in recent years is the evaluation of school textbooks and children's literature.
Several organizations have published criteria or guidelines for eradicating
biased material and choosing new books which are not wholly consistent with
cardinal educational values. Much admired in certain quarters are the
guidelines for the production of anti-racist and non-racist books published by
the World Council of Churches (WCC) in 1980. A 'good book' is defined as
one that satisfies the following 16 conditions:

1. Strong role models with whom third world children can identify positively are presented.
2. Third world people are shown as being able to make decisions concerning the important issues that affect their lives.
3. The customs, life-styles, and traditions of third world people are presented in a manner which explains the value, meaning, and role of these customs in the life of the people.
4. Those people considered heroes by the people of the third world are presented as such and the way they influence the lives of the people are clearly defined.
5. Family relationships are portrayed in a warm supportive manner.
6. Efforts of third world people to secure their own liberation are acknowledged as valid rather than described as illegal activities which should be suppressed.
7. The material is presented in such a manner as to enhance the self-image of the third world child.
8. The material is presented in such a manner as to eliminate damaging feelings of superiority—based on race—in the European child.
9. The illustrations provided are non-stereotypes and portray third world people in active and dominant roles.
10. The illustrations reflect the distinctive features of third world groups rather than presenting them as 'coloured Caucasians'.
11. The role of women in the development of third world societies and their impact on history is adequately presented.
12. The history of third world people and their role in developing their own society and institutions are accurately presented from their own perspectives.
13. The role of third world people in shaping historical events in their own country and in the world is accurately portrayed.
14. The content is free of terms deemed insulting and degrading by third world people.
15. The language of the people is treated with respect and presented in the proper rhythm and cadence.
16. The material has been developed by an author of recognized scholarship, valid experience, skill and sensitivity.

(Preiswerk, 1980, pp. 144–145)

I would have thought that the only conditions to be borne in mind when choosing (say) a new history, geography or social studies textbook for use in secondary school would be that it should be accurate and truthful, admit to the impossibility of telling the 'whole' truth, distinguish clearly between facts and its author's opinions, indicate the empirical basis for any judgements made and conclusions reached and, above all, encourage and assist pupils to think for themselves. A few of the conditions in the WCC list show some regard for accurate and truthful presentation of people and events, but most seem to be preoccupied with compensating for the stereotypical and ethnocentric portraits of an earlier generation of textbooks or with the likely effects of verbal and visual content on children's attitudes. There is also a distinct strain of 'strong' relativism and 'full-blooded' pluralism running throughout, while any concern for critical enquiry or independent thought is conspicuously absent. Altogether I can well envisage the implementation of such criteria leading to the production and adoption of narrowly conformist curriculum material. Consider, for instance, the first part of condition 4—'Those people considered heroes by the people of the third world are presented as such'. This condition seems to make no allowance for divergence of opinion among 'people of the third world' nor for the possibility that they might be as mistaken as anyone else in the assessment of their heroes.

ANTI-RACISM AND THE CURRICULUM

So far as curriculum development is concerned, there are very few examples of anti-racist teaching available that might enable one to evaluate its worth. The existing examples appear to combine multicultural content with the second of the three Stenhouse strategies for teaching about race relations—that of the committed teacher. Where the commitment is of an overtly socialist kind, the result seems to be indoctrination. This is not the place to embark on a philosophical disquisition about the necessary and sufficient conditions of indoctrination. I think I.A. Snook (1972) captured its essence when he wrote that it 'suggests that someone is taking advantage of a privileged role to influence those under his charge in a manner which is likely to distort their ability to assess the evidence on its own merits'. Stenhouse and colleagues also identified it in terms of attempts to 'evade', 'disarm' or 'subvert' the judgement of pupils.

Using Snook's definition as a yardstick one very clear case of indoctrination is the anti-racist material published in 1982 by the Institute of Race Relations (IRR). This consists of two booklets for use in secondary school—*Roots of Racism* and *Patterns of Racism*—which purport to foster children's 'critical judgement' by radically re-examining 'white society and history in the light of the black experience'. What they actually do is survey 'white society and history' from a Marxist viewpoint sometimes labelled 'black vanguardism' (Institute of Race Relations, 1982). This might please the compilers of the WCC checklist but is hardly compatible with recent trends in history teaching which stress the importance of nurturing children's capacities for independent historical enquiry. Another case of socialist indoctrination is the anti-racist humanities course developed by Chris Searle and colleagues in an East End secondary school whose outcome was the compilation of children's writing *The World in a Classroom* (Searle, 1977). I have criticized Searle's intentions and the IRR's materials elsewhere (Jeffcoate, 1979, 1984). I do not propose to do so again, but to look instead at another version of the Searle course provided by one of his colleagues, Bob Brett.

Somewhat oddly Brett (undated) states no socialist objectives and carries little of the Marxist flavour of Searle's prose. Indeed in some ways his version is decidedly liberal-minded—as, paradoxically, is Searle's—combining child-centredness with integrationism ('A harmonious multi-racial classroom is a living denial of racism'). But one is left at the end with a sense of unease. Brett makes much of the need to establish 'a reasonably relaxed and non-authoritarian relationship with the kids' in order to get them to 'open up' on race and racism, not however (or so it seems) because they should feel free to speak their minds in the classroom but for strategic reasons. He recognizes that there is only a slight chance of moving the minority of die-hards (those 'for whom being racist is central to their sense of their own value', referred to earlier in this chapter), and that working-class children alienated from school values can all too easily see anti-racism as just another set of institutional rules. Brett argues for the importance of building up 'a relationship of trust' so that the teacher can strengthen 'the anti-racism of those kids who are already anti-racist' and operate in the space provided by the 'many children' who 'have contradictory attitudes to race'. His targets are the racism of white children and 'the lies, distortions and half truths of the NF and the electioneering of right wing politicians and media' which are at least partially responsible. His strategy is to combat the first by exposing the latter through a process of 'persuasion'.

One cannot escape the impression that non-authoritarian classroom relationships and child-centred classroom techniques are advocated not so much because they are good in themselves as because they are likely to facilitate this process. In other words their value is perceived to be instrumental rather than intrinsic. One pauses too over whether persuasion, even if confined to rational argument and the exposure of lies and myths, is compatible with child-centredness and non-authoritarian classroom relationships. Children are, of course, entitled to expect to acquire knowledge at school, and to find irrationality and untruth challenged in the classroom, but there is more to the National Front, right-wing politicians and the media than misinformation and faulty logic. What of their opinions and attitudes? If Brett was, as he seems to have been, attempting to change opinions on political issues such as immigration control and race relations policy or alter attitudes towards ethnic minorities and their cultures, then he was 'taking advantage of a privileged role' to infringe his pupils' autonomy.

THE TARGETS OF ANTI-RACISM

A major problem confronting anti-racists is the absence of consensus on precisely what should be fought. About controlling and disciplining racialist behaviour there has never been any disagreement; and I have already expressed my bewilderment as to why some local authorities and schools should have thought it necessary to make such an issue of proscribing actions (personal abuse, bullying, physical assault) which, in my experience, have always been disciplinary offences. The same applies to the behaviour of teachers. I am equally puzzled why the NUT should have recently added to its codes of professional ethics and conduct a clause which states: 'A teacher should not behave in a racially discriminatory manner or make racist remarks directed towards or about ethnic minority groups or members thereof'. Does this mean that there has been a time when discriminatory behaviour and insulting remarks, at whomsoever directed, have not been contrary to these codes or that they are held to be reprehensible and punishable only when the content is racist? I would be interested in hearing the NUT's justification for either position.

I would also be interested in hearing ILEA's justification for its recent decree that staff who engage in racist activities will face disciplinary action. If this simply refers to racialist conduct at school, then I can only again wonder why such a decree should have been thought necessary. If, however, it refers, as I rather suspect it does, to members of staff joining racialist organizations and participating in their legal activities—attending meetings, distributing leaflets, going on demonstrations—then it is a breach of democratic rights and an early step on a totalitarian road. It will not be ILEA's only one, for it has also decreed that 'all pupils should be learning to identify, resist and remove racism'. This decree is, of course, guilty of the 'essentialist' fallacy—the misapprehension that there is something out there called racism waiting to be identified by those with sufficient knowledge and perspicacity. More to the point is the extraordinary presumption that an LEA is entitled to prescribe what pupils should seek to 'resist and remove'.

Political action, which is what it amounts to, is pupils' own prerogative. It is for them to decide how to respond to racism, depending on which sense of the word is intended. Herein lies the nub of the matter. Everyone might agree on the need to combat racism in the sense of racialist behaviour, and on the need to expose the irrationality of racial prejudice and stereotyping (differing only over choice of strategy). However, that still leaves a vast area of opinion and belief, represented by the ideology of racism in the original sense and the politics of immigration control and race relations, where, as often as not, it is not just a question of separating truth from falsehood, myth from reality, rationality from irrationality. If, during the course of the debate, and in possession of the relevant facts, some children argue that white people are as a group intellectually superior to black people, or come out in favour of repatriation and oppose racially mixed youth clubs or whatever, we have to accept that as their privilege. As concerned adults we may abhor these opinions. But, as teachers, our job is not to combat opinions we do not like but to uphold democratic principles and procedures.

REFERENCES

Brett, R. (undated) Charcoal and Chalk, *Teaching London Kids*, 11.
Davey, A.G. and Norburn, M.V. (1980) Ethnic awareness and ethnic differentiation amongst primary school children, *New Community*, **VIII** (1/2).
Davey, A.G. and Mullin, P.N. (1982) Inter-ethnic friendship in British primary schools, *Educational Research* **24** (2).
Home Office (1975) *Racial Discrimination*, Cmnd 6234, HMSO, London.
Home Office (1980) *Review of the Public Order Act 1936 and Related Legislation*, Cmnd 7891, HMSO, London.
Inner London Education Authority (1983) *Policy for Equality: Race*, ILEA, London.
Institute of Race Relations (1982) *Roots of Racism: Patterns of Racism*, Institute of Race Relations, London.
Jeffcoate, R. (1979) *Positive Image: Towards a Multiracial Curriculum*, Writers and Readers, London.

Jeffcoate, R. (1984) Ideologies and multicultural education in Craft, M. (ed.), *Educational and Cultural Pluralism*, Falmer Press, Brighton.
Milner, D. (1975) *Children and Race*, Penguin Books, Harmondsworth.
National Union of Teachers (1983) *Combating Racism in Schools*, NUT, London.
Preiswerk, R. (ed.) (1980) *The Slant of the Pen: Racism in Children's Book*, World Council of Churches, Geneva.
Searle, C. (1977) *The World in a Classroom*, Writers and Readers, London.
Snook, I.A. (1972) *Indoctrination and Education*, Routledge & Kegan Paul, London.
Stenhouse, L., Verma, G.K., Wild, R.D. and Nixon, J. (1982) *Teaching About Race Relations: Problems and Effects*, Routledge & Kegan Paul, London.

5

The 'Black Education' Movement

SALLY TOMLINSON

We believe black children aren't getting the best from local schools—they need the qualifications to get the jobs—and we aim to give it to them (Mel Chevannes, headteacher, Black Arrow Supplementary School).

Minority parents, on the whole, regard English state education as a potentially good education, and have high expectations of it. However, the disappointment many parents have experienced, the mismatch of their expectations with what schools actually offer, and the vocal dissatisfaction of a minority of parents, have led to demands from some parents and communities for additional, supplementary, and in some cases segregated, education. This chapter explores ethnic minority initiatives in education, and discusses the contradictions inherent in some of these initiatives. One initial contradiction should be noted: following the 1944 Education Act, the idea that state schools should provide a common and inclusive educational experience for all children has become increasingly accepted; but the existence of additional or supplementary schooling for minority pupils could be seen as undermining the aim of a common education for all pupils. However, it should also perhaps be noted that additional educational provision by parents or community groups now has strong support, as a result of government ideologies of self-help and commitment to increased parental choice and participation in the education process.

MINORITY INITIATIVES

There is a long history of the provision of supplementary and part-time education by minorities settling in Britain. In the nineteenth century,

Source: From Tomlinson, S. (1984) *Home and School in Multicultural Britain,* Batsford Academic, London.

supplementary schools for Irish children were organized, followed by Jewish, Polish and Italian Schools. A private Chinese school was established in London in 1934 (Ny, 1968) followed by part-time schools for Chinese children. A Greek Saturday School, also in London, was set up in 1922; and now, in the 1980s, when a quarter of all Greek Cypriots live in Britain[1] there is a strong commitment to retaining a Greek culture, and part-time schools exist in several cities. The Japanese are probably the most recent group to set up supplementary and private schools; the first opened in London in 1968, mainly to serve the children of Japanese businessmen temporarily in Britain, who will return to Japan and whose children need preparation for competitive Japanese examinations. But the most extensive development of supplementary and additional schooling has been provided by Caribbean, Pakistani and Indian settlers in Britain.

The reasons for the development of supplementary schools are complex, since they relate to the ways different ethnic groups wish to accommodate to the majority society, and the way this society reacts to different groups in terms of discrimination and exclusion. There is, for example, a distinct difference between schools set up to accommodate the children of Japanese or Iraqui business or diplomatic employees, and schools set up for Caribbean or Asian citizens in Britain.

A powerful motive behind the development of Jewish, East European, Greek, Chinese, Indian, Pakistani and Bangladeshi supplementary and additional education has been the desire to retain cultural identity, which in most cases is very strongly linked with the retention of a mother tongue and religious identity. Asian parents in Britain, in particular, face the problem of retaining a linguistic identity which will allow all generations within a family to communicate with each other, while at the same time ensuring that the children can operate in the language of the majority society.

Since the 1960s, additional education—religious, linguistic and cultural— has been offered to Muslim children at mosque schools, and to Sikh and Hindu children in gudwara and temple schools; and there has been a variety of community initiatives at the local level for instruction in mother tongue and culture (see, for example, Coventry, 1976). The EEC directive of the mid-1970s, charging member countries with a responsibility to ensure that mother tongue and cultural teaching were available to minority children, certainly stimulated debate in Britain as to how far such teaching should be provided in schools, and how far minority communities should take the initiative. The DES would seem to favour community initiatives. It did not accept that the EEC directive applied in its entirety to 'children whose parents are UK nationals with family origins in other countries' (DES, 1981b), but it did accept that there were implications for LEAs. Local Authorities, according to the DES 1981 Circular, should 'explore ways in which mother tongue teaching might be provided, whether during or outside school hours', and noted approvingly that in some areas provision is already made by minority communities. They considered that voluntary self-help schemes to retain language and culture should be encouraged by, for example, offering LEA premises to community groups for their classes. The NUT has also noted that 'voluntary provision already plays an important part in mother-tongue teaching and culture maintenance', but has stressed that co-operation between schools, home and community initiatives is vital, to ensure that minority children did not become overburdened (National Union of Teachers, 1982).

The overburdening of pupils attending mosque and temple schools after normal schools hours has always worried teachers. The National Association of Headteachers gave evidence to the Rampton-Swann Committee expressing such an anxiety, and pointing out that it was crucial for day and additional schools to understand and co-operate with each other.

Rex, reviewing arguments for and against the provision of minority languages and aspects of home culture in school, concluded:

> The maintenance of minority culture is best left to...adult members of the community involved, through supplementary education, unless in rare cases there are schools in which the 'subject' is understood and the place given to it in the curriculum is such that it does not imply inferiority (Rex, 1981).

While provision of supplementary education by Asian communities may be more related to aspects of cultural diversity, and the maintenance of a cultural identity, the provision of West Indian supplementary education is most strongly connected to the issue of equality of opportunity. As research has indicated, West Indian parents expect schools to teach their children much more successfully than they actually do, and are concerned and anxious that schools do not seem able to help their children pass the examinations increasingly needed for employment in Britain. Stone (1981) has pointed out that supplementary education is common in the West Indies, and the Northern School parents stressed that private tuition for children with particular school problems is also usual in the Caribbean.

At the moment, a minority of West Indian parents in Britain have resorted to these kinds of extra-educational provision, but increasingly supplementary education is being regarded as a desirable initiative.

THE 'BLACK EDUCATION' MOVEMENT

There has been sufficient criticism of the education system and enough initiative taken by some black parents, teachers, community workers and academics to be able to speak of a black education movement in Britain. The participants in this movement are united by a belief that schools designed for white, majority children cannot offer equal opportunities to black children, and that supplementary education is thus a necessity, but analyses as to why schools 'fail' black children differ. Some black educationalists point to the inability of urban schools to offer 'equal opportunity' to many white working class pupils, and refer to the poorer resources, less well qualified teaching staff, low teacher expectations, and low level exam courses offered in urban comprehensive schools. As Mel Chevannes has expressed it:

> Some parents believe the system works against blacks and working-class children, and are saying they are not going to take the sludge offered to them—they have higher ideals (Chevannes, 1982).

This view assumes that educational effort on the part of individual black parents and pupils will have a pay-off in terms of employment and social mobility. A more extreme view is taken by black academics at Birmingham University's Centre for Contemporary Cultural Studies. Carby (1983) has argued that many black parents had rejected the idea that schools could provide equal opportunities for their children by the late 1960s, and believed that state education was pushing young blacks into low-level education to ensure a supply of unskilled labour or an unemployed 'reserve army of labour'. While this extreme view may be held by some parents, and by some young black Britons, the *evidence* to date seems to be that most black parents still look to additional and supplementary schooling to enhance their children's life-chances.

The black parents' education movement has over the past eighteen years taken the form of diverse parents' and community groups, who have acted as pressure groups to campaign for improved education for their children, and have organized supplementary education. By 1965, the North London West Indian Association was becoming anxious about the number of black children sent to ESN-M schools, and in 1970 it lodged a complaint of racial discrimination with the Race Relations Board. The Board reported no evidence of an 'unlawful act', but at a Caribbean educational and community workers' conference held the same year, Coard spoke of the inappropriate way West Indian children were treated in British schools, that could result in them being 'made ESN' (Coard, 1972).

Protests about the over-representation of children of West Indian origin in ESN-M schools provided *the* major focus of concern for the black education movement during the 1970s, the over-representation of black pupils in disruptive units also becoming a crucial focus of concern by the late 1970s. It should perhaps be noted that central and local education authorities have never denied such over-representation, nor initiated any enquiries into the area (Tomlinson, 1982).

Haringey's black pressure group on education developed in 1977 from a united black women's action group, which had become increasingly worried by the low educational achievement of black pupils (Venning, 1983). The group, run as a collective, has consistently pressured the LEA and local schools about low achievement and disproportionate numbers of black children in ESN-M schools and disruptive units, and has campaigned against ethnic record-keeping in schools. The evidence of this group appeared to particularly influence the Rampton Committee's report on the education of children of West Indian origin (DES, 1981a). One of the most recent actions of the group has been to circulate all primary schools in East Haringey with a letter accusing heads of failing to provide efficient education: \

> The teaching of reading, writing, spelling and higher order language skills is your responsibility, and you appear to be failing miserably in that regard with a substantial number of your children, but specially black British children (Quoted in Venning, 1983).

Unsurprisingly, some of the actions of this group have antagonized schools and teachers.

Black women have been particularly active in setting up parent and community groups concerned with education. Aba Sindi, a black collective in Moss Side, Manchester, developed out of action by women, and now includes a supplementary school and a nursery school. Some local Community Relations Councils have worked with, or set up, parents' groups to pressure LEAs on educational issues. The Redbridge CRC worked with the Black Peoples Progressive Association to produce the report *Cause for Concern*, on the education of black pupils in Redbridge (1978); and Wandsworth Council for Community Relations worked with West Indian parents in 1979 to challenge the right of headteachers in ILEA to suspend black pupils or place them in disruptive units (Hughill, 1979).

BLACK SUPPLEMENTARY SCHOOLS

Actual numbers of black supplementary schools operating in Britain are difficult to estimate, particularly as some are very recent developments and may be operating without central or local educational authority aid or knowledge. The largest number of schools are to be found in the London area. ILEA reported in 1978 that it was giving grant-aid to two supplementary school projects, and recommended aid for a further ten projects. The reasons given for assisting the supplementary projects were that:

> —grant aid would respond to, and encourage, parental community interest in the children's education
> —the schemes encourage self-help and harness volunteer support
> —grant aid would assist the more disadvantaged sectors of inner city society to give their children the same help more fortunate sectors are able to provide
> —grant aid would enable the LEA to take a more active part in discussing methods and teaching materials with the sponsors.
>
> (ILEA Report 8689, 1978)

However, grant-aid from local authorities has been criticized by some black academics (e.g. Stone, 1981) as a possible way in which spontaneous self-help ideas will be lost, and a more rigid, hierarchic structure of 'alternative education' imposed.

The Home Office has also supplied money for black self-help projects, including supplementary education. Giles undertook a study of supplementary education projects funded under the Home Office self-help scheme in

1978, but his report was not published (it is available on request from the Home Office). Wellum (1981), in a survey of the library needs of pupils attending West Indian supplementary education schemes in London, included an appendix detailing supplementary schools she knew of. Her list included 41 such schools, although she did not claim accuracy or completeness. Research students at the North London Polytechnic worked in five of these schools and a report is available from the Polytechnic (Cronin, 1982). Stone, in Chapter Four of her book, *The Education of the Black Child in Britain* (1981), has documented four supplementary schools she visited in London, three being part of wider community projects; and Rex and Tomlinson (1979) described the Saturday and holiday school run by black community workers in Handsworth, Birmingham from 1974. Supplementary schools have been operating in Handsworth, Birmingham and Toxteth, Liverpool from the mid-1970s, and more recently in Wolverhampton, Manchester, Nottingham and other areas where there is a sizeable black population. Supplementary education is thus becoming an increasingly important aspect of the education of black pupils in Britain.

BLACK SEGREGATED EDUCATION

The idea that any form of racially segregated education should exist in British schools has always been repudiated by government and by educationists in Britain. The NUT wrote in 1967:

> It hardly needs saying that the Union, and we believe, the overwhelming majority of citizens of this country, would instantly repudiate any pattern of organisation which enshrined the principle of what is usually known as apartheid... that is, setting up of separate institutions or school organisations (NUT, 1967, p. 3).

This attitude has persisted. In 1980, when the Home Affairs Committee was gathering evidence for its report *Racial Disadvantage*, DES officials were shocked by the advocacy of separate black schools by representatives of the Liverpool CRC. An HMI spoke of

> ... the extraordinary advocacy of the witness from the CRC of black-only schools. This would seem to be a form of educational apartheid contrary to all we have been doing to build up a multiracial society (Home Affairs Committee 1981, evidence p. 433).

Nevertheless, the movement of white families from inner cities has meant that *de facto* segregation does exist in many urban schools, and these schools are the focus of some parental complaint. The 'failure' of schools to educate black children successfully has led to demands for official, separate black schools. Worrell, a black teacher, published an article in 1972 in which he advocated the education of West Indian pupils in all-black schools at the primary level, with pupils moving back into 'white' schools when they were academically as well qualified as their peers (Worrell, 1972). The West Indian Standing Conference, a group representing all West Indian organizations in the UK, proposed in 1977 that a black school should be set up as a pilot scheme. Such a school, it was suggested, should be centrally funded and inspected by DES, but 'managed completely by black teaching staff with all-black pupils... the curriculum would be slightly changed to accommodate the cultural and historical development of black children whose "identity problems" may be causing concern' (*West Indian World*, 1977).

A small number of black community workers also called for black segregated education at a conference meeting to discuss the Rampton Report (Rampton Conference, November 1981). They cited the opening of an independent black school, run by the Seventh Day Adventist religion, in North London, as an indication that black parents favour segregated education. This school was televised for a BBC 2 programme in November 1982, and the headteacher, Orville Woodford, was interviewed (Woodford, 1982). The school is run along traditional English 'grammar-school' lines, it is for black pupils only, fees are £700 per annum, and the 23 teachers are black. As one member of staff remarked:

> Staff identify with the children, they don't label black children's stages of development as a 'problem'. White teachers, no matter how sympathetic, are unable to do this.

The school has a uniform, strict rules which must be adhered to, and a 'subject-centred' curriculum. As Woodford noted,

> Black parents don't want black studies or multicultural education—that is for white children; our pupils need to be good at science, history, geography, and at what society thinks of as things of worth—it is like any good grammar school here.

The basis for black segregated education, then, is still a belief that such an education will ultimately help black children to succeed in an 'English' education, and acquire credentials which will prepare them for employment or further education and training in the majority society. The theme of equality of opportunity runs strongly through all demands for black supplementary and segregated education.

MUSLIM EDUCATION

The desire expressed by Muslim religious and community leaders, and a number of Muslim parents, for private or state-subsidized segregated education has quite a different base from West Indian desires for segregated education. Muslim parents are increasingly in conflict with a secularized co-educational Western educational system, and have become more vocal, particularly since the world-wide resurgence of Islam after the Iranian revolution[2] in asserting their own community needs and values. There is enormous scope for conflict and misunderstanding over this issue, as Islamic education is based on quite different principles and values to those of English education. In particular, Muslim parents question the materialistic and competitive basis of English education, the individualistic nature of learning, the way girls are educated, the predominance of Christian influence, and the separation of education from other aspects of life. These issues are tied in with a major anxiety which many Muslim parents feel: that their British-born children will move away from their faith, culture and influence. The Union of Muslim Organizations, an umbrella for all Muslim groups in Britain, has expressed the dilemma facing many parents thus:

> A major worry for Muslim parents is that their children soon begin to adopt English standards and ideas. They start to question not only traditional customs, but religious ideas which seem strangely alien to life in a Western materialistic society. Islam is not something which can be learnt and adhered to overnight, it must be lived, breathed and fostered, it cannot be separated from life itself.... Most Muslims acknowledge that Britain is a fair place to live... but it is hard to judge how possible it is to live as a Muslim in British society as a whole (UMO, 1975, p. 10).

For about twenty years, Muslim organizations in Britain have attempted to explain Islamic education to educationalists and persuade schools to recognize the validity of at least some Islamic ideas on education. The Muslim Educational Trust, registered as a charity in 1964, organized teachers to visit schools to teach religious education to Muslim children and explain Islamic principles to the schools, but it is probably true that for many years schools were unreceptive and have found great difficulty in reconciling English education and Islamic principles. Many schools serving Muslim communities become familiar with arguments over food, dress, P.E., swimming, dance and co-education for girls, and have only recently begun to relax school rules and accommodate to different standards. Few LEAs have gone as far as the Bradford Authority, who have issued comprehensive guidelines to schools on 'provision for pupils of ethnic minorities'—particularly Muslim pupils—which include for example a recommendation that halal meat be available at school lunch-times (Bradford, 1982).

Partly because schools were so unreceptive to Muslim principles, the demand for separate Muslim education, as distinct from the religious, cultural and mother-tongue supplementary education offered in mosque schools and private houses, has grown over the last ten years. A working party on the education of Muslim children was set up in 1974, following a conference on Islamic education in London. It presented its first report, *Islamic Education and Single-Sex Schools*, to the DES in 1975 (UMO, 1975). This paper set out to explain Islamic principles related to single-sex secondary education, and drew attention to the voluntary school arrangements laid out in the 1944 Education Act, which 'could enable Muslims to have separate schools'. In 1978, the National Muslim Educational Council was set up, and produced a set of papers on education (UMO, 1978) which further developed the case for separate state-subsidized Muslim secondary schooling, and the possible creation of a Muslim University in London. Despite advocating separate Muslim education, these organizations have been concerned to avoid the charge of segregation, recognizing that Muslim schools might be seen as racially segregated (UMO, 1975, p. 20), and have stressed that non-Muslims could attend such schools. The most recent development in Muslim demands for control over their own schools has been in Bradford, where the Muslim Parents Association has formally requested that five county schools (2 first, 2 middle and 1 secondary) be reclassified as voluntary-aided and the heads and school governors replaced by Muslims (Lodge 1983). The move has some support from the Bradford Council of Mosques, whose secretary was reported as saying: 'Parents would support a voluntary-aided Islamic school 100 per cent. The major problem is the education of our girls' (Lodge, 1983, p. 10). However, there are some signs that in Bradford, and elsewhere, the need for separate schooling is seen as less important now that state schools are beginning to take account of Muslim cultural, religious and dietary needs. The proposal for separate state schooling for Muslim pupils was also opposed by an association of young Asians in Bradford.

Muslim organizations have also considered setting up privately-funded independent schools—several are already in existence—and have at various times sought funding from Muslim countries overseas. Lodge reported in 1982 that Muslims in Batley, West Yorkshire, had appealed to the Libyan Government for aid to open a private primary school (Lodge, 1982). Malik, a community relations officer in Kirklees, has noted the 'considerable discussion and debate on the rise of Independent Muslim Schools in Kirklees and indeed elswhere' (Malik, 1982, p. 21).

Muslim desires for changes in the education of their children would seem, at present, to follow a continuum whereby some parents would be happy for their children to remain in existing state schools, providing more recognition were given to Islamic principles, but some, particularly religious leaders, would prefer voluntary-aided Muslim schools. Private Muslim schools are regarded as a last resort. The kind of changes many parents would like to see in state schools have been documented by Iqubal (Iqubal in UMO, 1978). He has written approvingly of the Sidney Stringer School in Coventry, where mother-tongue teaching, Islamic studies in single-sex annexes, freedom to withdraw children from Christian R.E. lessons, respect for dress, food and other cultural symbols, all add up to a school which 'takes due regard of the religious and cultural aspirations of [Muslim] children and parents' (UMO, 1978, p. 28). It is interesting that Iqubal is of the opinion that Muslim 'salvation' does *not* lie in the 'acquisition of professional qualifications or white-collar jobs' in the Western world, but in following Islam and Islamic principles of education.

The DES and some LEAs now find themselves in conflict with the demands Muslim communities are making, and are facing a series of dilemmas. There is no doubt that the 1944 Education Act allows for the creation of voluntary-aided religious schools. Dr Rhodes Boyson announced in Parliament early in 1982:

> The Government fully supports the very valuable part that voluntary schools play in our education system. They provide what many parents want for their children—education in a

maintained school but in an atmosphere which reflects their faith (*Hansard*, Vol. 18, No. 58, 16 Feb., Col. 128).

The present government is committed to increased parental involvement and initiative in education. However, it is debatable whether government had the Muslim religion or Muslim schools in mind when referring to voluntary schooling. Mrs Thatcher herself was reported in a recent interview as saying that in schools it was the state's job to express certain values and standards 'and these, I would say, are based inherently on Judaism and Christianity' (*The Sunday Times*, 27 February 1983, p. 34).

Some educationalists and Christian leaders have also expressed doubts about voluntary-aided Muslim schools. P.S. Dosanjh, who carried out the early study of Muslim parents and is currently a teacher in Birmingham, is of the opinion that Muslim denominational schools would be 'divisive and counter-productive' (Spencer, 1982a). The World Council of Churches also published a document in 1982 which noted that any school run for one denomination could be divisive, and used the example of Northern Ireland to illustrate potential conflicts (World Council of Churches, 1982). The Islamic education of girls also poses problems for English educationalists, since the whole thrust of girls' education in Britain for the past hundred years has been aimed at giving girls parity of opportunity with boys to enable them to aim for any occupation, rather than being educated for a separate sphere of life.

All in all, Muslim community and parental desires, even for educational change incorporating minimum Islamic principles in state schools, poses problems, and the notion of voluntary-aided separate Muslim schools is fraught with great contradictions. This issue probably emerges as one of the most difficult subsumed under the easy phrase 'multicultural education'.

SIKH EDUCATION

There have also been moves on the part of Sikh communities in Britain to establish separate Sikh schools, in addition to the supplementary education offered in the gudwara, to teach Sikh children religious principles, mother-tongue and culture. Unlike the Muslim communities, Sikh parents who desire separate schooling may be as interested in equipping their children with better qualifications to compete in Western society, as in providing cultural cohesiveness. Helwig, in 1979, documented a debate held in 1970 in Gravesend, concerning the setting up of a Khalsa (Sikh community) school. He described how, after the founding of a Sikh missionary society, two Sikh pupils were 'refused admission to an English school on the basis of thinly diguised discrimination', and the development of a Sikh school was discussed at a meeting of parents and community leaders.

A Sikh teacher in a Gravesend state school told the meeting:

Most Indian children are sent to the secondary school where they study until the age of 16. They are neither taught with exams in view nor given a real education. The enterprising children, encouraged by parents, may work for the CSE. Since their teachers do not take an interest, most of our children just bide their time until they can work in a factory or some comparable job. A few, who perform outstandingly, are put on G.C.E. 'O' level courses and have the door open to colleges (Helwig, 1979, p. 96).

Other parents gave their views that intelligence tests discriminated against Sikh children, that girls were 'taught that their parents were wrong in not giving them freedom', and that in English schools their children were losing all sense of a cultural and religious identity. One leader told the meeting:

We should instil pride in our religion and culture.The aim of education is to give identity and pride in one's heritage. The British education system is narrow and only concentrates on teaching students to fit into a Christian world, not a universal world (Helwig, 1979, p. 102).

However, other parents considered that the products of Khalsa schools would not 'fit into English society' and disagreed with separate schooling. In the event, no further steps were taken in the area, although the local gudwara did open a nursery school on its premises. Helwig commented that the Sikhs in Gravesend were seeking a niche for their children which would give them respectability, acceptance and equal opportunities with both Punjabi and English people.

Mukherjee has more recently documented the demand, made in 1978 by Sikh leaders in Southall, for a Khalsa school. The demand was influenced by the sale of a local state school to the Church of England, and the leaders sent money to the local council to buy a school in the same manner. The council returned the cheque with the comment:

There is a difficulty in showing the difference between a religious school, and a school which is tied to religion, to language and to race (Mukherjee, 1982, p. 135).

It is ironic after this comment that Lord Denning was subsequently to rule that Sikhs were not a racial group.[3] The Sikh leaders in Southall stated:

The realisation of a Sikh school is crucial not only for the continuity and survival of Sikhism, but is the only guarantee we can offer to our children of success in a hostile and pervasively racist society (Mukherjee, 1982, p. 136).

However, the community was not successful in setting up a Khalsa school. Some state schools, along with other social institutions in Britain, have been remarkably reluctant to accept the symbols of Sikhism. The turban has persistently been seen as a threat, in much the same way as some teachers regard 'Rasta locks' (Bidwell, 1978), and currently the wearing of the Kirpaan (ceremonial dagger) is causing problems in Leicestershire schools (*TES*, 11 February 1983).

SUMMARY

This chapter has discussed initiatives that some minority parents and community leaders have been making towards providing additional, supplementary, and in some cases separate, education of their children.

As a rather crude distinction, it was noted that while Caribbean parents tend to look to supplementary or segregated education as a means for improving their children's educational chances, Asian parents are more concerned that such education should enhance and develop cultural identity, and give support to parental and community values. Muslim parents who seek to ensure that their children are educated as far as possible in accordance with Islamic principles, are posing a series of problems for educationalists and for government, for which there are no easy answers. This issue demonstrates that the creation of a plural, multicultural society necessitates that the majority society accommodate to alternative values.

However, the distinction between the motives of different minorities in setting up alternative schools should not be pushed too far. Black supplementary or segregated schools, with black teachers and a curriculum which takes account of the children's needs, is probably a powerful force in enhancing a sense of worth and a 'cultural identity': at the same time, some Sikh parents, while wanting separate schools to support the preservation of their cultural heritage, are also concerned about equality of opportunity.

NOTES

1. OPCS, 1981. The invasion of Cyprus by Turkey meant that during the 1970s many Greek Cypriots emigrated from the island.
2. Naipaul (1982) has noted that since the Iranian revolution of 1980 and the resurgence of Islam as a proselytising religion, Muslims in many countries have felt more confidence in asserting their community and religious values.
3. This ruling was subsequently overturned by the House of Lords in the appeal case of *Mandla* vs. *Dowell-Lee*, 1983.

BIBLIOGRAPHY

Bidwell, S. (1978) *The Turban Victory*, London, Southall, Sri Guru Singh Sabha, Southall, London.
Carby, H. (1983) Schooling in Babylon, in Centre for Contemporary Cultural Studies (ed.), *The Empire Strikes Back*, Hutchinson, London.
Chevannes, M. (1979) The Black Arrow Supplementary School Project, *The Social Science Teacher*, Vol. 8, No. 4.
Coard, B. (1971) *How the West Indian Child is made ESN in the British School System*, New Beacon Books, London.
Cronin, A. (1982) *Black Supplementary Schools* (unpublished paper), Department of Sociology, Polytechnic of North London.
Department of Education and Science (1981a) *West Indian Children in our Schools*, A Report of the Committee of Enquiry into the Education of Children from Ethnic Minority Groups (the 'Rampton Report'), HMSO, London.
Department of Education and Science (1981b) Directive of the Council of the European

Community on the Education of the Children of Migrant Workers, Circular No. 5/81, DES, London.
Hansard Vol. 18, No. 58, 16 February, House of Commons, London.
Helwig, A.W. (1979) *Sikhs in England. The Development of a Migrant Community*, OUP, Oxford.
Home Affairs Committee (1981) *Racial Disadvantage*, 5th Report, HMSO, London.
Hughill, B. (1979) Wandsworth Parents' Group, *Issues in Race and Education*, No. 21.
Inner London Education Authority (1978), *Grant-Aid to Supplementary Schools*, Report No. 8689, ILEA, London.
Lodge, B. (1982) Libyans ask for cash aid, *Times Educational Supplement*, 29 October 1982.
Lodge, B. (1983) Putting their money where their faith is, *Times Educational Supplement*, 25 February 1983.
Malik, S.K. (1982) *A Response to the Report of the Kirklees Interdirectorate Working Party on Multi-Ethnic Kirklees*, Dewsbury, West Yorkshire.
Mukherjee, T. (1982) Sir Guru Sabha—Southall in Ohri, A., Manning, B. and Curno, P. (eds.), *Community Work and Racism*, Routledge & Kegan Paul, London.
National Union of Teachers (1967), *The NUT View on the Education of Immigrants*, NUT, London.
National Union of Teachers (1982), *Mother Tongue Teaching*, NUT, London.
Ny Kwee Choo (1968), *The Chinese in London*, OUP, Oxford.
Rampton Conference Report (1981) (opened by Sir Keith Joseph to debate the Rampton Report), *West Indian Children in Our Schools*, DES, London.
Redbridge Study (1978), *Cause for Concern, West Indian Pupils in Redbridge*, Redbridge and Black Parents' Progressive Association, Community Relations Council.
Rex, J. (1981) Equality of opportunity and the minority child in British schools, Paper presented to conference on the Rampton Report, University of London Institute of Education, London, November 1981.
Rex, J. and Tomlinson, S. (1979) *Colonial Immigrants in a British City—A Class Analysis*, Routledge & Kegan Paul, London.
Spencer, D. (1982a) Asians look to mainstream as only long-term answer, *Times Educational Supplement*, 12 March 1982.
Stone, M. (1981) *The Education of the Black Child in Britain*, Fontana, London.
Sunday Times (1983) Interview with the Rt. Hon. Mrs. M. Thatcher, Prime Minister, 27 February 1983.
Times Educational Supplement (1983) Ceremonial dagger poses problems, 11 February 1983.
Tomlinson, S. (1982) *A Sociology of Special Education*, Routledge & Kegan Paul, London.
Union of Muslim Organisations of United Kingdom and Eire (1975) *Islamic Education and Single-Sex Schools*, UMO.
Union of Muslim Organisations of United Kingdom and Eire (1978) National Muslim Education Council—Background Papers UMO.
Venning, P. (1983) Menacing warning sent to Haringey heads over exams, *Times Educational Supplement*, 11 February 1983.
Wellum, J. (1981) *Survey of Library Needs of Black Supplementary Schools*, North London Polytechnic, London.
West Indian World (1977) Call for black schools, 6 October 1977.
Woodford, Orville (1982) Interview on 'Ebony', BBC TV, 17 November 1982.
World Council of Churches (1982) *Christians and Education in a Multi-Faith World*, WCC.
Worrall, M. (1978) Multiracial Britain and the Third World—tensions and approaches in the classroom, *New Approaches in Multiracial Education*, Vol. 6, No. 3.

Sex Discrimination and Educational Change

6

The Winning of the Sex Discrimination Act

MARGHERITA RENDEL

In this paper I examine the processes by which the Sex Discrimination Act (SDA) was won: how this proposed legislation was put on the public agenda, who the actors were, what methods they used and so on. Winning equality legislation for women has not been easy. It took nearly a century to win the suffrage, and well over half a century to win equal pay legislation. But the campaign for non-discrimination legislation resulted in the SDA in less than 10 years. What made the difference? The success in winning the SDA is the more remarkable in that women have relatively little access to decision-makers and the media.

Theories of agenda-building can help to answer this question. Cobb, Ross and Ross (1976, p. 126) defined agenda-building as 'the process by which the demands of various groups in the population are translated into items vying for the serious attention of public officials'. They identified three broad models of agenda-building: (1) outside initiative, where the initiative for action comes from groups who are 'outsiders' in political processes; (2) mobilization, where the initiative is taken by insiders and effective action depends on mobilizing public opinion; and (3) inside access, where the initiative comes from inside and success depends on keeping the initiative out of public gaze.

The history of the SDA falls into four periods: (i) the period before 1968 and the renewal of the women's movement shows the general context; (ii) from 1968 to 1974 influential public opinion was converted to legislation; (iii) April 1974—December 1975 saw the passage of the Act; (iv) since the passage of the Act, the difficulties of implementation reflect in part the success of the opposition.

Specially commissioned for this volume, © 1985 The Open University.

BEFORE 1968: THE GENERAL CONTEXT

In the 1960s in Britain, as in the United States, there was plentiful evidence of women's dissatisfaction with the home-bound life expected of married women, and of their desire for at least part-time work with satisfactory child-care arrangements available. There was also a shortage especially of teachers and nurses. By the middle and end of the 1960s, prejudice and discrimination were increasingly recognized as barriers to women's education, employment and equality. Women's position in social security was criticized, as were income tax provisions, women's legal status in family law and discrimination against women in public life. The wealth of writing of this period laid the foundations for demands for equality and for questioning notions of a special domestic function for all or the majority of women.

Steps to mobilize influential support had been taken well before 1968. The Executive Committee of the National Council for Civil Liberties (NCCL) was persuaded that discrimination against women was a problem that deserved the Council's attention by the three women who carried out a survey of job advertisements in the quality Sunday papers (Rendel, 1964). A Fabian Society Study Group set up in November 1964 on the initiative of the present author agreed at the first meeting in January 1965 that the possibility of adapting U.S. anti-discrimination legislation for British use should be investigated, and in its report, *Equality for Women* (1968), so recommended (pp. 41–43).

1968–1974: THE IMMEDIATE CONTEXT: OUTSIDE INITIATIVE AND MOBILIZATION OF OPINION

Concern for improving the status of and opportunities open to women became respectable in 1968, the fiftieth anniversary of the winning of the Parliamentary franchise for some women and the fortieth anniversary of winning it for all women. Eminently respectable, polite, lobbying organizations held anniversary meetings as well as publishing pamphlets (for example, The Status of Women Committee meeting in March 1968, Fawcett Society meetings). This anniversary movement coincided with Human Rights Year which included women's rights. In this way, the idealism and aspirations expressed in the UN Declaration had a practical and educative effect for women.

During this period, mobilization continued apace and women acquired 'insider' support. Such support made it possible, first, to put anti-discrimination legislation on the public agenda, and, second, to get legislation through Parliament. To gain inside support an influential minority and a wider circle of interested persons and groups had to be won over. But in 1968 very few knew about or understood anti-discrimination legislation. Influential support had to be won for unknown measures to deal with a largely unrecognized problem. Who had to be convinced, by whom, and by what processes were the difficulties overcome? And it is also often asked: why legislation to deal with a social evil that, it is said, can be solved only by changes in attitudes?

The reasons for legislation were summarized by the Race Relations Board in 1967 (First Annual Report, para.65):

1. A law is an unequivocal declaration of public policy.
2. A law gives support to those who do not wish to discriminate, but who feel compelled to do so by public pressure.
3. A law gives protection and redress for minority groups.
4. A law thus provides for the peaceful and orderly adjustment of grievances and the release of tensions.
5. A law reduces prejudice by discouraging the behaviour in which prejudice finds expression.

Further reasons are that government departments and local authorities may, in general, carry out only those functions for which they have statutory authority and that they are under an obligation to comply with the law. Anti-discrimination legislation can therefore legitimate policies which without it would face much greater opposition.

Those to be convinced are those with power to carry through legislation, that is leading politicians in a governing party, and the wider circle includes women's groups and organizations and the Women's Movement. In Britain, virtually all legislation is government legislation or passed with government support. Since 1945, all governments have been single-party governments. It is sometimes argued that controversial issues (for example, homosexual law reform, abortion law reform, abolition of capital punishment) are most likely to succeed in Parliament if they have all-party support. Such issues almost invariably receive support from some members of all parties, but the majority of supporters are usually members of the Labour Party. The very few Private Members' Bills that are passed are either very simple and short, or receive substantial government help or at least tacit support. Private Members' Bills therefore often serve to demonstrate support for measures. This was the case with the Anti-Discrimination Bills. Anti-discrimination legislation is not simple. Therefore, gaining inside support was crucial to winning the SDA. As we shall see, this support came from the Labour Party in spite of considerable opposition from Trades Union Congress (TUC) at first. Support also came, as might be expected, from some women's organizations, for example the Fawcett Society, and from the Women's Liberation Movement. Women's Liberation groups began to form early in 1969. Rowbotham (1972) traces the links with the Trade Union movement and left-wing and student groups. Early participation by some leading trade unionists in the National Joint Action Committee for Women's Equal Rights (NJACWER) helped to legitimate discrimination against women as a serious issue in left-wing groups, which, in Britain as elsewhere, have often been extremely hostile (see, for example, Mitchell, 1971, pp. 74–86). However, at the first conference of the Women's Liberation Movement held at Ruskin College, Oxford, in 1970, a motion supporting anti-discrimination legislation was carried by only a fairly small majority.

In November 1967 the Parliamentary Labour Party (PLP) and the National Executive Committee of the Labour Party (NEC) established the Study Group on Discrimination Against Women. This Study Group included several MPs, a member of the TUC General Council, the Chief Women's Officers of the TUC and of the Labour Party, members of the National Labour Women's Advisory Committee and of the National Joint Committee of Working Women's Organizations, the present author, and Anthony Lester, a Fabian who subsequently became Roy Jenkin's Special Adviser at the Home Office. The Study Group was chaired by Douglas Houghton, recently Chancellor of the Duchy of Lancaster with a general responsibility for the reform of social security. Much of the early work of the Study Group was devoted to the reform of social security legislation, crucial to establishing married women who took paid work as independent individuals rather than as mere dependants of their husbands. The specific recommendations, published in 1969 as *Towards Equality*, followed broadly the lines suggested in *Equality for Women* (Rendel and others, 1968) and were discussed with Labour Ministers. They appeared with modifications in the Study Group's evidence to the House of Lords Select Committee on the Anti-Discrimination Bill and were followed by legislation.

At the Study Group's meeting on 13 June 1968, two months after the publication of *Equality for Women*, Anthony Lester suggested that the American and Canadian legislation on equal pay and equal opportunity in employment should be examined. The Group next discussed the matter nearly a year later, was unsympathetic to an anti-discrimination board and favoured strengthening other machinery such as the Central Training Council. Papers on anti-discrimination legislation[1] were discussed in the winter of 1969–70. Opposition came overwhelmingly from the TUC, which noted the doubt in some sections of the Labour Party about the value of the Race Relations Act 1968 and argued that girls' education in science subjects should be improved by coeducation, and that the first Secretary for Employment should use her powers to direct Industrial Training Boards (ITBs) to ensure that girls were included in schemes approved by the Boards, that local authorities should provide child-care facilities and nursery schools, that discrimination against pregnant women under the Redundancy Payments Act should be ended, and that the proposed unfair dismissal legislation should ensure that women were adequately protected. The TUC at this stage was relying on piecemeal measures to protect women.

By 1972 the TUC had changed its position. This change was almost certainly brought about by the evidence of increasing segregation of men's and women's work following the Equal Pay Act.[2] By this segregation, employers were able to keep women's wages down. Such an outcome would have two effects damaging to both the Labour Party and the Trade Union movement: women, the fastest growing group of Trade Union members, would be disadvantaged by a Labour Government's legislation; and the chances of women's labour undercutting men's wages would be increased (for example, by employers sacking men and replacing them by lower paid women). The TUC therefore supported anti-discrimination legislation. There were two problems about organization. Should the same board deal with women as well as racial minorities and should complaints of discrimination be dealt with by the ordinary courts, by industrial tribunals or by special tribunals. The Study Group came to no conclusion and in its final report in November 1972 stressed the importance of passing comprehensive anti-discrimination legislation, either by conferring wider and stronger powers on the Race Relations Board or by creating a new body.

Meanwhile, every year from 1968 onwards, backbenchers introduced anti-discrimination Bills. The Bills, modelled on American legislation and very short and simple, all dealt with discrimination in access to education, training and employment and provided for the establishment of an anti-discrimination board. Education was rightly seen as important to employment opportunities and as being influenced by them. Other provisions included in some Bills dealt with access to public places, the advertising of vacancies, membership of professional bodies and Trade Unions. The main emphasis was on employment, including employment in educational establishments. All the Bills in the Commons were initiated by Labour members. All were supported by members of all three parties and, in the Lords, also by a former Lord Chancellor and two Bishops. However, much of the work in Parliament was done by Labour members of both Houses and by the Liberal Peer, Baroness Seear. Outside Parliament, the predominant share was undertaken by members of the Labour Party, trade unionists, the Fawcett Society and activists in the Women's Liberation Movement, although important contributions were made by independent and non-party organizations and groups as well as by individual Conservatives.

The crucial developments took place in the 1971–72 and 1972–73 sessions. By this time, there was again a Conservative Government. The Bill was talked out of the Commons (28 January 1972), but a government-sponsored wrecking amendment moved by Baroness Sharp was defeated in the Lords (14 March 1972). The Bill was then referred to a Select Committee empowered to hear evidence—an unusual procedure. During the two sessions, the Select Committee received a mass of evidence, not all of it published, from a variety of organizations and individuals on the extent of discrimination. This evidence astounded the male members of the Committee.

Evidence was received from several educational bodies. That submitted by the Association of Education Committees and the Committee of Vice-Chancellors and Principals (personal communication) has not been published. None was received from the University Grants Committee or, as far as

Margherita Rendel

I am aware, from any of the teaching unions. The Institute of Careers Officers (21 November 1972) gave examples of discrimination; in oral evidence, the two women witnesses clearly favoured legislation, but their man colleague feared it would be ineffective and did not on the whole support it. The National Union of Students (NUS) (12 December 1972) set out full evidence of discrimination against girls and women in education and strongly supported legislation. The Deans of Medical Schools (13 February 1973) expressed surprise at and ignorance of the well-documented facts that many medical schools imposed quotas, often as low as 15 per cent, on the admission of women students and that some required higher 'A' level grades from women applicants.

Evidence about education and training was submitted by non-educational bodies. Most of this evidence demonstrated the extent of discrimination against girls at school and against women students (Political and Economic Planning,[3] 20 June 1972; Women in Media Group, 4 July 1972; National Council of Women, 11 July 1972; Edward Bishop, 1 August 1972; TUC Women's Advisory Committee, 24 October 1972; Women's National Commission, 14 November 1972; Labour Party Study Group, 14 November 1972;[4] National Joint Committee of Working Women's Organisations (NJC), 21 November 1972; Margherita Rendel, 21 November 1972; Eileen M. Byrne (unpublished)). Some of the evidence, especially that from PEP and the NUS, stressed the importance of sex-stereotyping as a way of discriminating against girls. Other evidence, notably that from the CBI (25 July 1972), claimed that women's restricted employment opportunities and low pay resulted from the education girls received. The Engineering Employers' Federation (10 August 1972) stressed the long training required for draughtsmen.

The Select Committee had before it evidence of discrimination against women, both overt and covert, in virtually all aspects of the public domain, but particularly in employment. The majority giving evidence supported the principle of legislation[5] and a number suggested improvements in the drafting. The opposition to the principle of legislation was mostly implied rather than explicit. The government departments (Employment, 6 June 1972; DES, 13 June 1972; DHSS, 13 June 1972; Civil Service Department, 29 June 1972; Home Office, 24 October 1972) argued that legislation was unnecessary or inappropriate because, they said, there was no discrimination in their departments or the services for which they were responsible or, in the case of the Home Office, claimed that jobs in their services had by their nature to be restricted to one sex or the other.

Those opposed to legislation, the CBI, the Engineering Employers' Federation and the Conservative Party Women's National Advisory Committee (12 December 1972) claimed respectively a broader measure was needed, legislation was unnecessary or education was what mattered. However, later there was opposition to including education in such legislation.

By the summer of 1972 the Select Committee most needed evidence that legislation would work. This evidence came from Irene Johnson, Commissioner for the Public Service Commission of Canada, Margherita Rendel, and Sonia Pressman Fuentes of the US Federal Equal Employment Opportunity Commission and Catherine East. Irene Johnson's evidence (29 June 1972), showed the contribution that legislation was making towards a changed and more equal climate of opinion in Canada. Margherita Rendel's evidence gave an account of the American legislation, summarized the deficiencies of existing British legislation, suggested improvements to the Bill and showed how a strengthened Bill would help to end discrimination. This evidence was followed by detailed, specific evidence from Sonia Pressman Fuentes[6] and Catherine East. Thus the Select Committee received the evidence to convince it that legislation was feasible and could be effective.

The Select Committee proposed substantial amendments to the Bill, drafted with expert assistance from a Parliamentary draftsman, in the light of the evidence received (Special Report, 27 March 1973). The Bill was renamed the Sex Discrimination Bill. Clause 4 relating to education defined the forms of discrimination more precisely and provided an exception for single sex schools and colleges, but would have banned the establishment of new single sex institutions. The Second Special Report (18 April 1973) reviewed the evidence concluding unanimously in favour of legislation, explaining the reasons for the amendments and the relationship of the Bill to existing legislation. In the debate on 14 May 1973, the Conservative Government unexpectedly gave an undertaking (col. 619) to hold consultations and present a Bill in the next Session. The Report of the Committee was agreed to.

Meanwhile, the Bill was again introduced in the Commons and again talked out in the face of opposition from both sides so strong that the Labour Chief Whip offered Opposition time for a further debate on the Bill (2 February 1973, col. 1886). As a result, the Government found time for the Bill to be reintroduced on 14 February 1973 when it passed its Second Reading without a division. This Bill also was referred to a Select Committee. The evidence submitted to the Lords was made available to the House of Commons Select Committee, which also received a considerable volume of additional evidence. The Committee confined the oral evidence to civil servants and Ministers from the Home Office, the Department of Employment, the Department of Education and Science and the TUC.

The most extraordinary evidence was probably that given by the officials of the Department of Education and Science and its Secretary of State, Mrs. Margaret Thatcher, who all denied the existence of discrimination in the education system in spite of the evidence given to the Lords.
The Secretary of State said:

> It is alleged that rather fewer girls take scientific subjects than boys. I think that is so. It may be so because rather fewer girls want to take scientific subjects . . . or because . . . they do not

find that they have sufficient employment opportunities at the other end...girls who want
to go on to take advanced degrees may want a commercial career in the City. Undoubtedly
there are not many employment opportunities open to them.... In view of the great debate
for relevance as far as education is concerned, there would seem to be some sense in most
girls doing some of the domestic science subjects, and there is not the time for everything in
the curriculum (Q. 259, 15 May 1973).

The Committee noted in its Report (29 June 1973):

There remains a widespread feeling that discrimination between boys and girls exists in the
educational field however difficult it may be to identify. The view that differences exist in
opportunities and facilities available and in assumptions about future careers for boys and
girls is strongly held. We believe that the Department of Education and Science have been
complacent in its reaction to these criticisms. We recommend that the Secretary of State
should establish machinery to keep these areas of concern under regular review (para. 17).

The powers of the proposed Anti-Discrimination Board in the original Bill
were extremely limited. They were expanded by the House of Lords Select
Committee, in spite of some opposition, to include the power to conduct
investigations in the absence of a complaint (Clause 10) by analogy with
Section 17 of the Race Relations Act 1968, and in addition to conduct general
enquiries into the position of men and women in particular industries and
organizations. In its Report, the Commons Select Committee recommended
that the Board should have such powers (para. 40), a recommendation
carried on the vote of the Chairman—the only occasion on which he voted
against his party and with the Labour members.

Throughout the period, the work of informing relevant outside opinion
(women's organizations, Women's Liberation Groups) about anti-discrimination legislation continued through public meetings, processions, committees and the circulation of papers. Women booked halls, advertised meetings
and took collections to cover the hire charges. Meetings in London, Cardiff,
Glasgow and Edinburgh were organized around the visit of Catherine East,
who also received attention from the media.

The work of the Select Committee in the Lords and in the Commons and
the publicity surrounding that work compelled the Government to change its
position. But if the Government had really supported legislation, it would
surely, as various members of the Select Committee suggested in the Lords
debate on 14 May 1973, have taken over the Bill as a Government Bill.

The Government's Green Paper, *Equal Opportunities for Men and Women*
of September 1973, far weaker than the Lords' Bill, proposed enforcement
machinery only for discrimination in employment, including employment in
educational establishments. As regards admission to educational establishments and courses, the Secretary of State was proposing to consult with those
responsible for the education service at all levels. As regards Local Education
Authorities,

The Ministers would not hesitate to use their powers if it appeared that the appropriate
authorities were exercising or proposing to exercise any of their functions in a
discriminatory way (para. 3.4).

The powers chiefly are those conferred by section 68 of the Education Act 1944, but in paragraph 4 of Appendix 2, the Document states: 'there is no central control'. The Government believed that those responsible for the educational service would respond to 'guidance and encouragement' from the proposed Equal Opportunities Commission. Individuals were to be allowed to bring cases to the Industrial Tribunals, and the EOC would be able to make local enquiries and propose to the Government the holding of an investigation (para. 4.5) but would not have power to compel the disclosure of information or the appearance of witnesses except in relation to *'employment investigations approved by the Government'* [my italics] (paras. 4.2 and 4.6). Admission to courses and the treatment of pupils and students in educational establishments would therefore be excluded from investigation.

The great majority of individuals and organizations commenting on the Consultative Document expressed deep dissatisfaction, both with the weakness of the enforcement machinery and with the failure to deal adequately with discrimination in education.

That the proposals were weak and would have been ineffective does not detract from the achievement of shifting the Government's point of view. In six years, an idea which had been thought unimportant had become a matter of Goverment policy. This result had been achieved by skilful and determined manoeuvring in the Labour Party and Parliament, by individuals and organizations and by effective public demonstrations. The Conservative proposals were a rearguard defence aimed at preventing consolidation of the change which had been brought about.[7] 'Reformist' tactics had changed the terms of the debate. It was no longer a question of whether to have legislation, but what sort of legislation. Sex discrimination legislation was on the political agenda.

1974–75: THE PASSAGE OF THE SEX DISCRIMINATION ACT

After the fall of the Conservative Government in March 1974, the Labour Government and its Home Secretary, Roy Jenkins, were determined, for reasons of political expediency as well as principle, to carry strong sex and race discrimination legislation through Parliament. The Equal Pay Act, a Labour measure, was in danger of becoming meaningless as some employers further segregated men's and women's work, thereby defeating the purpose of the Act. On the other hand, the new Government had only a tiny majority, and equality is a principle to which lip-service is paid but was not (and is not) regarded as one of the great principles which should have priority in implementation. Ministers and governments are constrained by the opinions and prejudices of colleagues in government, in the Party and on the backbenches, by the abilities and sympathies (or lack of them) of civil servants, by the support or hostility of influential pressure-groups, by the shortage of time in government departments and in Parliament (persuading people takes time and energy), and by the conventions of the Constitution and views about the proper way to do things.

First, the Conservative proposals had to be replaced by effective ones: to achieve this, considerable resistance within the civil service had to be overcome[8] (personal communication). The White Paper, *Equality for Women* (Cmnd. 5724), declared the legislation would include employment, education, goods, facilities and services and access to public places (para. 93). The EOC would have wide powers and be responsible for the strategic attack on discrimination (para. 110). The EOC would have power to assist individuals, to undertake formal investigations on its own initiative, to compel the production of documents and attendance of witnesses in all formal investigations, and to issue non-discrimination notices (paras. 110–123). Individuals would be able themselves to take cases to the courts or tribunals and the unsatisfactory conciliation procedure of the Race Relations Act 1968 (Rendel, 1976) was largely abandoned. The burden of proof was, unusually, to be on the defendant to justify alleged discrimination (para. 86). Comments were invited on this statement of Government policy. Since some of these proposals would arouse strong opposition, it was crucial that a wide range of organizations should express support in order to strengthen the bargaining power of the Government.

The Bill, published in March 1975 after the Labour Government had been returned to power in October 1974 with a substantial majority, showed a number of changes from the White Paper. The concept of indirect discrimination was included following the visit of Roy Jenkins and Anthony Lester, his Special Adviser, to the United States. This provision has proved to be of great importance and can sometimes deal with the effects of past discrimination. Representations about this had been made to the Home Secretary by the Labour Party in December 1974 (personal correspondence). The other gain was a very small measure of affirmative action for training (Clause 41). Also the EOC was empowered to issue codes of practice by the Race Relations Act, 1976.

A price had to be paid for the inclusion of education in the Bill: first the EOC would not be able to issue non-discrimination notices in relation to education, and second, complaints about education would have to be referred to the Secretary of State in the first instance. The period during which the Secretary of State could consider such complaints was reduced from 4 months to 2 months in the Lords on the initiative of Baroness Seear,[9] who defeated the Government (17 July 1975, cols. 1377–1382). Repeated attempts to reduce the period to 3 months had failed in the Commons.

The most serious loss between the White Paper and the Bill was that the burden of proof was put back on the complainant, as a result, it is said, of the determined opposition of some of the Law Officers (as well as of others). All attempts by the feminist lobby to get it back on the defendant on the analogy of the unfair dismissal legislation was unsuccesssful. Among the most important unsuccessful amendments were the regular collection of statistics to monitor possible discrimination, and contract compliance, in spite of strong support for it (Rendel and others, 1968; evidence to the House of Lords from the Labour Party and from S.P. Fuentes; Special Report to the House of Commons Select Committee, Appendix 14).

Inevitably the Bill did not go as far as many of its supporters would have liked. Since there was substantial opposition within the civil service, the Special Adviser had to select which issues to fight on. To succeed, he had to get the time of the very busy Home Secretary and brief him; this was impracticable except on the most important issues. It would have been impossible to deal with sex-stereotyping in school curricula and textbooks, both because of the administrative opposition it would have aroused and because the content of education was not at that time a subject open to direct ministerial intervention, still less to statutory intervention.

Women MPs and peers briefed by feminists and members of the Labour Party Study Group worked for improvements, but the Bill was attacked by some Women's Liberation Groups for not dealing with social security, income tax, family law and much else besides. While the women were right to stress the importance of these matters for women's equality, they were out of touch with the realities of legislative processes and the structure of the statute book.

PROBLEMS OF IMPLEMENTING THE SDA: THE CONFIDENTIAL AGENDA OF THE OPPOSITION

When the Act came into effect on 29 December 1975, only the Chairman and Vice-Chairman of the EOC had been appointed. The part-time Commissioners, appointed on that day, saw themselves as representing established interests and not as advocates of sex equality (Byrne and Lovenduski, 1978, pp. 143). Many senior staff arrived in post during 1976. The EOC was therefore quite unprepared to take advantage of the 'Personchester' jokes to which its location in Manchester gave rise. Although the Commission met only monthly, it refused to delegate to the very committed staff, who were told to leave their 'feminist hats' at home (Meehan, 1982, p. 15). It seems the Commissioners saw the EOC as an impartial body adjudicating, as it were, on discrimination, enquiring, persuading and offering helpful advice, whereas the staff saw it as a campaigning body, whose function was to end discrimination. Since the EOC was set up to make a strategic attack on discrimination (*Equality for Women*, 1974, para. 81), the staff were closer to the *intentions* of the White Paper than the Commissioners. The EOC is handicapped further because of uncertainty about how far the supervisory power of the sponsoring department, the Home Office, extends in relation to staffing grades, expertise and numbers (Meehan, 1982)—and finance—total budget and virement (personal communication).

The courts tend to lack an understanding of the nature of discrimination and its effect on women's lives, and many judges and members of Tribunals are unsympathetic to the purposes of the legislation.[10] Both the Lord Chancellor's Department and the Central Council of the Industrial Tribunals have resisted all offers of training to explain the purposes of the Act; judges fear that training might lead to bias in interpreting the law (Report of the Working Party on Judicial Training and Information, Chm. Lord Bridge, 1978).[11] The courts have been unduly sympathetic to the applications of those resisting formal investigations.[12] Differences in procedure make legislation of this kind much more difficult to operate in this country than in the United States (Rendel, 1976; Byrne and Lovenduski, 1978; Meehan, 1982). Even in the industrial tribunals with their cheap and relatively simple procedure, the proportion of cases won is abnormally low and the number of cases declining (*Employment Gazette*, 1983, Vol. 91(4), pp. 165–169). The *Whitfield* case was the first education case to have come to court.[13] Helen Whitfield had to apply specially if she wished to take craft subjects. The judge did not compare her treatment to that of boys who were automatically allowed to take craft subjects but to the fact that boys had to make a special application in order to take home economics—a fallacious comparison—and held that Helen was unduly influenced by her feminist mother. The EOC refused to support an appeal. Girls were frequently denied access to craft and technical subjects. The EOC has shown LEAs that such practices are unlawful and provided advice on how to comply with the law. Many LEAs have instructed their schools accordingly. This work led to a formal investigation into the training of craft, design and technology teachers. Litigation cannot therefore be used as a measure of the effectiveness of the Act.

The agenda of those opposed to sex discrimination legislation was (and is) to weaken the implementation of the Act. The Ministers and others favouring the legislation were transitory but the opposition has permanent and easy access to power and to those in powerful positions. The appointment of Commissioners is in the hands of the Home Office and through them the choice of senior staff can be influenced. The Home Office determines the resources of the EOC, a policy body situated 200 miles away from the majority of those it needs to influence, with a resulting increase in administrative costs. The opposition's success in preventing the amendment of the Bill to include the compulsory provision of statistics ensures that the EOC will always have difficulty in establishing the *prima facie* case needed for justifying formal investigation. The EOC has not received strong public support from the Women's Movement for necessary reforms, nor has it sought such support.

CONCLUSIONS

Why did the Labour Government bring in strong sex discrimination legislation? It has been suggested that the impending EEC Directive on equal treatment was the principal reason. However when the Labour Government came to office in March 1974, it was already committed to strong sex discrimination legislation and had produced its proposals by September 1974. The EEC draft Directive was less advanced; when the House of Lords European Communities Sub-Commitee considered the draft Directive on 30 April 1975, it noted the absence of exceptions and assumed that the Directive would not pass in its existing form. In fact the Directive was accepted on 9 February 1976 and allowed governments 30 months, i.e. until August 1978, in which to pass appropriate legislation or other measures (Article 9(1) of the Directive). While it would be wrong to assume that the likely policies of the European Communities had no influence on a government and a minister committed to Europe, it seems unlikely that European Communities policy was the decisive factor in passing strong legislation in 1974/75.

Other reasons for legislating were more powerful and more immediate. As already noted, the Equal Pay Act was failing, the TUC had already been converted to the principle of legislation in 1972, there was support for legislation within the Labour Party, and the Select Committees had enabled outsiders to mobilize and demonstrate support. It is almost inconceivable that such legislation would have been passed, had the TUC been hostile to it. Perhaps because sex discrimination legislation had not been taken very seriously, no strong overt opposition was demonstrated at that time; indeed the evidence of government departments and some other bodies was perfunctory. Another reason for legislating was the conviction on the part of Roy Jenkins and his Special Adviser that the race relations legislation had to be strengthened. It would have been politically damaging for the Labour Party to have done nothing for women while strengthening race relations legislation. The Sex Discrimination Bill provided, as it were, a test-bed for the Race Relations Act, 1976. By the Spring of 1974, in the immediate aftermath of the Select Committee Reports, people had been prepared for such legislation; consequently it would not arouse as much opposition as it would have done at an earlier period (or a later one when people had forgotten). In other words, the time was ripe.

Nonetheless, social change does not occur untouched by human hands; still less is this the case with political change. A few key individuals (perhaps about half a dozen) were determined to get legislation. They had access, through past work, membership of relevant committees, voluntary and political organizations to those who were able to get legislation through and those who would be able to mobilize the support of their organizations. Some individuals wore several hats, provided links between and contacts, information and resources for a variety of groups.[14] Assiduity, persistence, knowledge of procedure and timing were necessary to make the best of these resources and contacts, as well as flair and imagination in catching the public eye.

I have suggested that those hostile to anti-discrimination legislation did not take it very seriously. Arguments in favour of discriminating against those who are qualified and willing are unlikely to command public support. But the opponents of sex discrimination legislation did not need to enter the public debate. They were (and are) defending the status quo; they had easy and established access to civil servants and politicians and they could pray in aid traditional liberal principles in opposing, for example, placing the burden of proof on the defendant in a discrimination case or requiring the collection of statistics on the numbers and distribution of women employed in individual firms and institutions. Gaps of this sort, so easily defensible, have undermined the effectiveness of the SDA (and of the RRA 1976).

Nevertheless, the SDA has provided an important legitimation of women's demands for equality. The EOC has provided a great deal of material justifying equality and recommending practices tending towards equality, especially in education. There has been a change in atmosphere that has had a diffuse effect in widening women's opportunities, and a proportion of women have gained more pay, jobs and promotion. These are all net gains.

The SDA was won by a combination of those inside and those outside. Such a combination has developed in some LEAs between teachers, the Authority and women's groups. If the gains of the SDA are to be consolidated, extended and defended, such combinations are widely needed. The attack on women's equality will at this stage necessarily be oblique.

NOTES

1. By Anthony Lester and the present author.
2. For example, the First Report on the Implementation of the Equal Pay Act, 1970, of the Office of the Manpower Economics, 1972.
3. An independent research body, now part of the Policy Studies Institute.
4. This influential evidence earned a *Times* leader headed 'A Great Social Evil'.
5. Mrs Irene Johnson, Commissioner of the Public Service Commission of Canada, Anglican Group for the Ordination of Women (4 July 1972), National Council of Women, Institute of Personnel Management (25 July 1972), Edward Bishop, MP, National Union of Journalists, Margherita Rendel, whose evidence was supported by the British Federation of University Women, The Fawcett Society and the Home Office Issues Task Force of the Fabian Society, the TUC Women's Advisory Committee, the Labour Party Study Group, the NJC, the NUS, Ms Sonia Pressman Fuentes of the EEOC and Ms Catherine East. Sir Roy Wilson of the Race Relations Board did not express a view either way, but drew attention to the importance of drafting.

6. It was significant that she was invited, because of lobbying by M. Rendel, in her personal capacity, rather than as representative of the Equal Employment Opportunity Commission, USA.
7. The Government's proposals are reminiscent of the ploy by which in 1918/19 the Women's Equality Bill was superseded by the much more limited Sex Disqualification (Removal) Bill. See Simon Trotter (1981) who discusses these two Bills in Women Teachers and the Marriage Bar, unpublished MA dissertation in Rights in Education, University of London Institute of Education.
8. Governments of all parties have complained of difficulty in getting civil servants to implement their policies.
9. Ably briefed by Dr. Eileen Byrne, then Deputy Chief Education Officer of Lincoln City.
10. A reading of the judgements makes these conclusions inescapable.
11. This point was made also in a letter to the present author from the Lord Chancellor's Department. The EOC has attempted to organize training on more than one occasion.
12. The Commission for Racial Equality (CRE) faces similar problems; see, for example, *London Borough of Hillingdon* vs. *CRE* [1982] IRLR 424 and *In re* Prestige p/c [1984] i RLR 166.
13. *Whitfield* vs. *London Borough of Croydon & Woodcote High School* [1979] unreported. The CRE also has had very few education cases.
14. The All-Party Parliamentary Equal Rights Group, Chairman, Mr. Edward Bishop, MP (now Lord Bishop), was particularly helpful.

REFERENCES

Byrne, P. and Lovenduski, J., Sex equality and the law in Britain, *British Journal of Law and Society*, Vol. 5 (2), pp. 148–165, 1978.
Cobb, R., Ross, J-K. and Ross, M.H., Agenda-building as a comparative political process, *American Political Science Review*, Vol. LXX (1), pp. 126–138, 1976.
Labour Party Study Group, *Towards Equality, Women and Social Security*, Labour Party, London, 1969.
Labour Party Study Group, *Discrimination Against Women*, Opposition Green Paper, presented to House of Lords Select Committee, Labour Party, London, 1973.
Meehan, E., Implementing equal opportunity policies, *Politics*, Vol. 2 (1), pp. 14–20, April 1982.
Mitchell, J., *Woman's Estate*, Penguin Books, Harmondsworth, 1971.
Rendel, M., Do women have trouble getting jobs, *New Society*, London, 27 August 1964.
Rendel, M., *et al.*, *Equality for Women*, Fabian Research Series 268, London, 1968, Repr. 1972.
Rendel, M., Law as an instrument of repression or reform, in Carlen, P. (ed.), *The Sociology of Law*, Sociological Review Monograph 23, Keele, 1976.
Rowbotham, S., The beginnings of women's liberation in Britain, compiled by Wandor, M., *The Body Politic*, Stage 1, London, 1972.

7

Equality or Equity?
a European Overview

EILEEN M. BYRNE

My destiny must be out there someplace
Malena, aged 20, Sweden, 1975

The thoughtful speaker was Malena, at the end of her training for technical work in the Saab factory as part of the Swedish experiment established in the late 1970s to open up the 'male' labour market to women and to abolish the sex cleavage we have so insidiously inherited (Advisory Council on Equality Between Men and Women, 1979). She had been asked to look ahead ten years to her new future, as part of the evaluation of the trainees, their families and their workmates. Malena had welcomed the skilled work and higher pay—but she and her husband Urho, for whom home was 'a safe and secure island', were now *both* having to reconcile home, work, and a career which led to more than work in a Saab motor factory, to enable them both to have an equal opportunity to develop as leader worker, as parent, as citizen, as creative and individual people. When the children begin to arrive, it will still, however, be Malena who will tend to perceive a long-term alternative of part-time or no work for herself, as the mother, even long after the children are semi-independent. Does not Urho, her husband—and the father—have an equal right to the full pleasure of being a homeparent, of part-time work, of fuller fatherhood for at least part of his children's formative years?

The conference for which this paper was prepared, was essentially indeed about the destiny that the education service shapes for Malena's successors and their need for an unfettered, less conditioned preparation for a changing work ethic, for swifter social changes and for increasing participa-

Source: From Marland, M. (1983) *Sex Differentiation and Schooling*, Heinemann Educational, London.

tion by women in government and politics and economic development, if we are to survive in peace and stability not only into the new decade, but into the new century which is just around the corner for today's children.

Jacqueline Nonon, head of the Women's Bureau of the Social Affairs Directorate of the Commission of the European Communities, puts it more bluntly. If we go into the twenty-first century without women's full potential, we shall fail: a rendezvous with history will be missed.

> La transition d'un siècle à l'autre ne se
> fera bien qu'avec les femmes; si elle se
> fait sans les femmes, elle sera ratée: ce
> sera un rendez-vous manqué avec l'histoire (Nonon, 1978).

This chapter aims to provide a backcloth against which the detailed studies on sex differentiation in education can be seen, rather than to attempt to deal in detail with current European trends. There are three broad themes against which I believe work both at national levels and in the school, college, or local environment can helpfully be set.

First, the *concept* of equality itself—how to achieve consensus on what in fact we are aiming for; how this matches the international agreements to which we among others are as a nation committed; and what the implications are for educational planners and educators. What is equality? What is equity?

Secondly, the direct and inescapable responsibility of national governments to create and *carry out with resources* a coherent national plan for the achievement of educational equality. In the United Kingdom, the biggest single hindrance in my view to the achievement of sex equality, regional and rural equality and racial equality, is the persistent refusal of government, central and local alike, to take any accountable responsibility whatever for ensuring the achievement of a national plan of education; for a common core to which every child has a right and for which every educator has a duty to provide; and for a national minimum standard of resources and good practice which is not dependent on the accident of the area of residence or on the particular philosophy of the head of the institution. There is a point at which defence of uncontrolled educational autonomy is in danger of becoming a hidden anarchy of non-provision. Unlimited delegation leads to planned inequality.

Thirdly, the need to understand better the full educational implications of the dual role for both sexes, and the concurrent urgency of curriculum reform for a compulsory common-core education for both sexes, for parenthood, or rather for a range of kinds of *family living*—since at any one time, by no means a majority of our citizens live in family situations with responsibility for young children; yet all will need the art of homemaking and of maintaining personal and satisfying relationships.

Fourthly, the need for positive discrimination (or for what is known in Scandinavia as 'temporary preferential treatment') in the curriculum as in training and in the labour market, if both sexes are to catch up with the areas of knowledge and skills in which we now know there to be major sex differences—whether these are innate or conditioned. The 1970s have seen some important innovative work in this field, and the decade has also seen a major international commitment to these principles, which a later section develops briefly.

EQUALITY OR EQUITY?

The weakness of the United Kingdom's attempts to achieve an educational equality programme is our consistent refusal to define precisely what we mean by equality. Even the Sex Discrimination Act is highly ambiguous in the wording of its education sections, and we have yet to see any proposals for amending the Act for which many of us have pressed now for many years. But most other countries have nailed some form of flag to the mast and their educators have, therefore, clearer guidelines which are reflected in their curricular planning, and which they can then monitor.

The *Shorter Oxford Dictionary* defines *equality* as 'the condition of being equal in quantity, amount, value, intensity, etc...the condition of being equal in dignity, privileges, power', under which definition the planned provision for girls in most of our schools can hardly yet be said to be equal. *Equity* on the other hand is defined as 'the quality of being equal or fair; impartiality', and is clearly set in the context of jurisprudence. This is a useful distinction, and a reflection of the major trend of the 1970s, which have seen a reassuring strengthening of legal, formal and constitutional equity both at national and international levels. Although formal equity does not necessarily result in factual equality in the 'Monday morning' situation of a classroom or staffroom, it is an essential prerequisite to a national acceptance of the need for rigorous monitoring and real application of what otherwise remain 'progressive' principles held by an enlightened minority. It follows that equality and equity are complementary rather than alternatives.

But how do we define equity (in the legal sense) or equality (in the Monday morning sense) for curriculum and planning? Uniformity or equivalence?

EQUAL MEANS THE SAME

As long ago as 1967 the United Nations declared that equal means the same in its declaration to abolish sex discrimination:

All appropriate measures shall be taken to ensure to girls and women, married or unmarried, equal rights with men in education at all levels, and in particular: (a) equal conditions of access to and study in educational institutions of all types, including universities and vocational, technical and professional schools; (b) the same choice of curricula, the same examinations, teaching staff with qualifications of the same standard and school premises and equipment of the same quality whether the institutions are coeducational or not; (c)

equal opportunities to benefit from scholarships and other study grants; (d) equal
opportunities for access to programmes of continuing education, including adult literacy
programmes and (e) access to educational information to help in ensuring the health and
well-being of families (United Nations, 1967).

In common with most of my European colleagues, I believe without
reservation that *equal means the same*—that is to say, the same across sex, race,
rural and urban children of similar abilities and aptitudes. It does not mean
uniformity across the full ability range, or across genuinely different interests
or personalities. But it does mean uniformity for boys and girls in all that
relates to the common core of knowledge, skills, attitudes and experiences
without which no one will survive in happy and fulfilled, efficient and
adaptable adulthood. And that means that this country has to cease its
comfortable evasion of the difficult but not impossible task of defining that
common core—a task that even the Third World countries, leave aside our
continental colleagues, have not been afraid to face. I am not, let me stress,
talking of uniformity of detailed curricular content to the last historical date
or set book, nor uniformity of teaching methodology, but that, for example, a
core of homecraft and parenthood, technology and manual skills, mathematics and a balanced core of the sciences, at least one creative art, a modern
language, and so on, should be the essential heart of the same compulsory
education of all girls and all boys—taught together—up to the school-leaving
age.

Or does equal mean equivalent? While the EEC commentary on the
Community's Directive on Equality in Employment speaks of 'comparable'
general education for both sexes and of 'comparable' educational and
vocational guidance, the actual Directive later sharpens this to equal
opportunity in access to all forms of vocational training. Article 3 of the
Directive indeed makes it clear that equal access and standards must be
according to ability and aspiration, not to sex.

The implementation of the principle of equal treatment in regard to vocational training
*requires access to all levels of general education, initial and advanced vocational training and
retraining*, in accordance with their abilities and aspirations, whether such education and
training is provided in institutions or on the job.
In order to enable women to obtain the qualifications assuring them equal opportunities of
employment, member states shall take steps to ensure that equal standards and level of
general and technical education and vocational guidance, initial and advanced vocational
training and retraining, shall be available *without discrimination based on sex*, or on marital or
family status (Commission of European Communities, 1975).

The view that equal means the same, was reinforced by the European
Ministers of Education of the twenty-two Council of Europe countries who
met in June 1979 at The Hague to debate equality of education for girls and
women at their biennial Conference. This complemented the major initiative
of the Commission of the European Communities whose earlier commissioned study of equality of education for girls, completed in 1978 (Byrne,
1979), was also presented to the Standing Conference as one of four expert

studies for debate. The Ministers declared in their published statement after the conference that: 'Because sex is becoming, and should become, less relevant in the distribution of functions in adult life, the educational choices offered to boys and girls should be the same' (Standing Conference of European Ministers of Education, 1979). Ministerial speeches from the widest variety of countries also endorsed the need for boys and men to take a full and equal share in domestic responsibility, childrearing and family life, and for the *common* curriculum, therefore, to educate both sexes in this expectation.

PLANNING FOR NATIONAL EQUALITY

This heightens again the difference between the United Kingdom and its continental neighbours. Most other countries have defined some form of national plans for coherent action over the next decade at least. These without exception incorporate some definition of equality and of its educational implications for action—which European Ministries across the water are prepared actually to endorse with resources. As long ago as 1972 the Nordic Ministers of Culture and Recreation, for example, surveyed the whole effect of the education structure on sex roles in educational materials and on the sex distribution in teacher training and employment, and defined equality: 'Equality between men and women is taken to mean equal worthiness of the sexes and a balanced distribution of duties within the family, at work and in public life' (Nordic Council for SCEME, 1979). Within the Nordic group, Norway and Iceland have in fact clearly legislated for sex equality in education: 'Women and men shall be equally entitled to education. Instruction in schools and other educational establishments shall be organised to *ensure* equality of the sexes. Textbooks and other teaching materials shall not discriminate against either sex' (ibid.).

Note that they are not controlling or necessarily defining which books to use on which course, but are prepared to monitor unsuitable books in general. But where in the United Kingdom education service is there a single point of accountability—central or local—that would ensure equality, even after declaring it as a constitutional right? The Sex Discrimination Act only guarantees a form of equality for those in coeducational schools and excludes children in single-sex schools and the early test cases from 1978–80 under section 22 of that Act, aimed at establishing that equal curricula between the sexes means identical curricula equally offered and accesible, were lost in a welter of ambiguity.

In Sweden the whole education and training system has now come to be based on a concept of equality in which women and men are expected to enjoy the same rights and freedoms within all life areas. The educational goal set before teachers is 'a whole and indivisible human being' evolving out of the dialectic between sensibility and objectivity, strength and weakness: rejecting sex-polarities on any 'normative' basis.

Denmark has also endorsed this in its recent major and seminal education discussion document for the 1990s called *U90*, in declaring that for the education service

> True equality resides precisely and expressly in the full respect of the originally given, unpredictable difference... accordingly an equality-oriented education becomes an individual-oriented education and not its contrast...
> All citizens must be entitled to the same amount of education... the same resource-equality... if not in the young years, then he or she must be *entitled* to retrieve the situation later on, for example, in the form of a preferential right of adult education (Danish Ministry of Education, 1978).

The key word is *entitled.* Moreover, in all the Scandinavian countries, both boys and girls are given an identical education throughout the first cycle of secondary education, including both homecraft and textiles and the manual and technical basic skills.

The Danish authors of *U90* take for granted (as we do not) that equality means a *political* commitment—it is in their view essential that 'politicians establish that equality-orientation *is a central aim* that must be respected from first to last in the educational system', as a counter-weight to the traditional teaching matter and behavioural patterns in school which 'conceal remnants of previous periods' views on human beings and culture which were greatly characterized by acceptance of sex and class differences' (p. 120). In Denmark, of course, the cross-timetabling of 'boys' subjects' and 'girls' subjects' was abolished in 1970 by amendment to the education legislation, and both sexes are now taught woodwork, textiles and homecrafts in coeducational classes. The 1975 Danish Schools Act made further proposals to counteract traditional sex roles.

The Dutch have also set out on their road, with a published discussion document sketching out the future of the education system as a whole over the next twenty-five years, *Contours of a future education system.* It defines equal opportunity not as uniformity, in the sense that again the individual differences between children must be recognized, but declares that equality requires equal options regardless of sex or social class in order to develop ability, interests and skills to the full, and that 'extreme care must be taken that a certain basic level and knowledge and skill... is attempted and indeed obtained' (Second Chamber of the States General, 1974–75)—and this common core is for both sexes.

The Dutch point of departure, however, is that educational establishments must themselves be made capable of giving form and content to changes in their own environment and work, and with Dutch logic and consistency, it is spelt out in a government memorandum that facilities must be 'related to each other and geared to each other in a *support structure*'. The Contours Memorandum identifies six means of doing so—all of which are accepted as a government responsibility for their enabling:

New approaches to initial teacher training
Refresher and retraining in new interchangeable sex roles
Innovation in guidance services (for teachers and students alike)
Improved research
Curriculum development
Improved dissemination of knowledge, information and expertise.

This proposed support-structure has a dual purpose—not only to support and service educational establishments, but also to enable the government to pursue a nationally coordinated policy to make innovation and reform a widespread reality in The Netherlands.

In outlining these examples of national planning for educational reform which includes sex equality and social class equality, I am not necessarily arguing that all is well in those countries, nor that *de facto* equality will automatically follow *de jure* declarations of intent—or equity. There are still worrying sex differences in The Netherlands (in particular), in Scandinavia and elsewhere as their Councils and Commissions for Equality regularly diagnose. Nevertheless, at least they are tackling the problem. Moreover, it is significant that it is those countries in which national standards *ensure* that both sexes follow a common-core curriculum up to 15 years, which includes homecraft and technical/manual crafts for both sexes, which also show a substantial and statistically significant proportion of girls entering non-traditional or 'male' areas of further education, training or work on leaving school. (That is to say, Germany, France, Denmark, Sweden.) I do not believe that this is coincidental.

The European Ministers at their 1979 Conference in fact also came to an unusually firm public conclusion that formal equality was indeed not enough. When they examined the mass of evidence presented to them on what girls could actually study and what they actually achieved, they went on record for the first time as recognizing now that 'formal equality in education has not been sufficient to achieve factual equality of opportunity for girls and women either in the educational system or in the life for which it is a preparation'. They recommended that there was a need for every country to commit itself to 'A *new overall policy* designed to *ensure* that in all areas of life equality between the sexes becomes a reality' and spoke of a 'coherent approach' in all forms of education—institutionalized and otherwise—which would complement social and employment policies for equality in each country. This is perhaps the more important where a country is starting with a major inherited problem, like the United Kingdom and The Netherlands. The Netherlands has a sex-segregated vocational training system and one of the lowest proportions of women in economic activity, in politics or in leadership of the industrialized countries. The United Kingdom has a secondary-school system in which girls may need to go to court to be allowed—let alone encouraged—to learn manual crafts or technical drawing.

The Ministers recognized in particular that 'Future European society cannot afford to leave a large part of its potential not fully realised'—that is the female potential—by the under-representation of women in scientific and technological work and in the leadership of education. This clearly means altering school and college practices—now and not at the millennium—to delete cross-timetabling on grounds of sex. It means developing compensatory programmes in mathematics and technical education, and *it means that government must devote resources for this.* We cannot continue to say that equality and the development of the brains in half the population of the United Kingdom in the fields most vital to our economic competitiveness with other industrialized countries, must wait 'until we can afford it'. Economically, we must find the resources or we will cease to be a viable nation. The corollary of the cumulative evidence available at international levels is that the United Kingdom must begin to accept some form of national, centrally defined and determined, policy standards of equality and of *resourced,* policy-based educational objectives, if we are to keep pace with our international neighbours.

EDUCATION FOR THE DUAL ROLE

The relationship of the sharing of the dual role by both sexes to curriculum planning has been well debated and well rehearsed. It is encouraging that a third principle endorsed in the European Ministers' formal statement issued after their 1979 conference, declared that

> Education systems should . . . also prepare *all pupils* for the sharing of domestic and parental responsibilities and equip girls as well as boys to earn an independent living, to cope with the technical elements of practical life and to participate in democratic decision-making and public life.

This has major implications for curriculum reform, for alternative methods of timetabling, and for the future of any single-sex school or college which perpetuates the existing mutual exclusivity of domesticity for girls and technical education for boys.

But culturally, as well as economically, we are facing regression, not progress, on the educative and social acceptance of the right of girls to full investment in training, in work, jobs, careers, whether or not they marry. All over Europe, female unemployment is rising at several times the rate of male unemployment. All over Europe, girls are relatively protected in academic, school and general education—but they are losing the battle for fewer and scarcer places on vocational training courses, except those traditionally reserved for women. Again, it is significant that those countries who have taken decisive steps to enshrine in their constitutions declarations of the rights of both sexes, happen also to be those with the most positive policies of training for women, of positive discrimination and of the highest proportion of women in leadership and non-traditional roles. Finland, for example, categorically defines the right of gainful employment as the main criterion of female independence, and Finland has the highest proportion of women

MPs in its government. It so happens that it has also produced some interesting analyses of the conflict of the dual role and of women's participation in decision-making. Riitta Auvinen's review of Finnish women in leadership endorses strongly that it is only when women begin *successfully* to compete with—and overtake—men, that pressure is exerted socially, publicly and personally by criticisms that women fulfilling a dual role—but not their male colleagues—are neglecting their (often by then well-grown) families (Auvinen, 1975). But when men have in turn competed with women in entering 'female' fields of training and employment, and then take over the leadership (as all over Europe the trend now shows they do) their 'threat' to women does not evoke parallel accusations of paternal deprivation and family neglect as their top posts lead them to be absent from the home more, and home even later in the evenings.

Evidence from Austria confirms the double standard of society's expectations of working women and working men. The Austrian microcensus of June 1973 into family relations examined the participation rates of wives, husbands and children in five main household tasks: shopping, washing dishes, cleaning the home, shining shoes and doing household repairs. The figures are differentiated by workdays and Saturdays, and by full-time working, part-time working and not working at all (that is, not in paid employment). Men, whatever their or their wives' working status, were only prepared to take from 13 per cent to 15 per cent of the shopping and shining shoes; and at no point more than 5 per cent of home-cleaning (even when men were part-timers). Men's acceptance of 85 per cent of work in household repairs (intermittent and essentially a sporadic weekend task) is in no way comparable with the daily and constant dishwashing, home-cleaning and shopping of which women did 85 per cent. Interestingly where women in paid employment *were* able to shed some household tasks, the statistics show that the work was transferred to the *children* and not to their husbands (Gaudart, 1975). This is confirmed by the evaluation of the Swedish experiment referred to below.

SCHOOLS AND PARENTS

This double standard cannot alter until teaching staff in schools and colleges, educate boys as well as girls to the idea of mutual freedom, mutual merit, mutual right and mutual respect outside the home as well as within it. This means working with parents, of course. One important study from the Délégation à la Condition Féminine in France examined the role of mothers and fathers respectively in the guidance of their daughters and their sons in school subjects, career expectations and attitudes to their future roles in the family. The results will probably not surprise readers. Forty-four per cent of the parents thought that educational failure was serious for boys; none thought it mattered for girls since 'La fille a la remède de se marier'—girls could always fall back on marriage. The 31 per cent of parents who thought that choice of job and career was *more* important for boys and not important for girls, said candidly that it was because they believed that the boy *should* become the head of the family and the breadwinner, and that education for girls was mainly a matter of their personal development. One out of two of the mothers in the survey, perceived the essential characteristic of 'feminine' employment to be sporadic, unimportant, not requiring high qualifications and limited to the 'extended maternality' spheres regarded as 'suitable', that is teacher, nurse, child care (Délégation à la Condition Féminine, 1978). A second French research study confirms these findings. Parents from the Pas de Calais region with children in the fourth year of secondary schooling, expressed much more anxiety about sons' career choices than about daughters. The replies from the parental sample showed also a quite different pattern of parental expectation for girls and boys, a 'manifestation of an extremely strong interiorisation of the stereotypes of the masculine and feminine roles in society, that is of course, of the objective possibilities of the masculine labour market and its feminine homologue' (Beture, Département Socio-Economique, 1974). And 'même en rêve, les filles ne s'autorisent pas autant d'ambition que les garçons' ('Even in imagination, girls show less ambition than boys') (ibid).

THE CONCEPT OF POSITIVE DISCRIMINATION

The need of the education and training services to counteract attitudes as well as inadequate skills and knowledge—in both sexes of course, but, for me, with decisive priority for girls until they catch up!—is an important development which we have only begun in this decade, so far behind our transatlantic colleagues. Article 14 of the International Convention on human rights outlaws discrimination based on *unfounded* and alleged differences solely on grounds of sex. This applies (as does my 'equal means the same' principle) to all that relates to *basic* rights—the core, the foundation, the right to progression and to all educational services which are a key to unlocking further doors.

But we have accepted for centuries that to enable some who are handicapped either by innate disability, or by social disadvantage, or by accidental and temporary problems (illness, long-term absence from schooling) to achieve equal opportunity, they need extra remedial help—not a different base always, but additional compensatory education. Why is this so controversial when it is directed at girls and women? Remedial language help tends to benefit more boys because their language development is less advanced at a given stage. Why has the concept of remedial numerical and scientific education, which happens to benefit more girls, taken over a century to gain respectability? No European country has yet committed itself to a numeracy remedial programme equivalent to its language remedial programmes.

The Federal Republic of Germany launched a major national programme of compensatory programmes of education and training to train girls and women in mathematical, scientific, technical or craft skills for non-traditional 'male' employment, and evaluated the results by professional and sociopedagogic research teams—the result of which was debated together with analyses of similar programmes in Sweden, France, etc., at a World Congress mounted by UNESCO in 1980. The Germans had already declared their belief in full equality, but it should be said that the real motivation behind the new programme was their recognition that, with a declining birth rate, they will be desperately short of skilled technical labour by 1985. But so will Great Britain. Where is our parallel programme? The MSC and TSD programmes so far have been distinguished principally for the number of women on secretarial courses! The numbers on non-traditional training are infinitesimal, and again form no part of any definable national plan involving the Department of Education and Science in collaboration with the Department of Employment and the Department of Health and Social Security.

Similarly the Swedish 'temporary preferential treatment' programme writes a resources cheque which we do not. The Kristianstad project to train women in technical fields usually regarded as 'male', has now been evaluated in terms of effect on families as well as workplace (Advisory Council on Equality Between Men and Women, 1979). Sweden gives major subsidies to firms who train women in 'male' fields, for equal means the same in Sweden's social goals. Companies seeking regional aid must also now ensure that at least 40 per cent of the jobs *newly created* as a result of regional aid will be reserved for each sex, with back-up special training if need be. There is not space here to deal with the full findings of the Kristianstad survey, but let me dispel one myth of 'family deprivation' alleged to arise when mother works and takes on a dual role. The Swedish researchers themselves became conscious that the very way they framed their questions to the mothers on the effect on their children *presumed* the presence of problems by 'treacherously and biassedly' formed questions. But although the mothers were, therefore, 'on the alert, prepared at any moment to take the blame upon themselves (rather than on the absence of good solutions to child care and the negative effects of restrictive hours of work)' (ibid., p. 126), nevertheless, four positive and substantial results recurred in many families:
1. Children became more independent
2. Children had more (good) contact with fathers
3. Children took more responsibility for themselves and helped out more in the home
4. Children benefited materially from the improved family income.
Interestingly, the children's answers tended to confirm the recorded parental opinions.

Understandably, the Ministers at the Conference were more divided on affirmative action programmes, given the different social, cultural and demographic characteristics of the different countries. Nevertheless, the Ministers' formal statement does accept that actual 'measures should be taken in support of those women, or men, who wish to make non-traditional choices as regards subjects, courses or educational institutions'. A range of possibilities were mentioned in the Ministers' declaration (Standing Conference of European Ministers of Education, 1979). These included:

> special *information* and *guidance* and special *incentives* to encourage the entry of women to traditionally male-dominated technical institutions and vocational courses;
> *compensatory curricular* programmes for girls and women, e.g., in technical subjects, mathematics, and in politics and civics for adult women;
> action to *encourage* employers to accept candidates of either sex regardless of tradition.

While accepting the inclusion of the qualifying words preferred by some countries of 'where national situations permit', the Ministers still took a generally supported view that 'positive discrimination, where national situations permit, might help in the short term to overcome the minority position of women in many areas of activity, including public administration, employment, policy within education, and those fields where women are conspicuously under-represented.' Within the overall concept of positive discrimination—or affirmative action—there was also Ministerial concern, reiterated in their statement, that special attention should be paid to the needs of groups at risk through 'compound disadvantage'—for example:

> migrant women
> women seeking their first employment
> women wanting to return to employment after a prolonged break.

THE INTERNATIONAL ORGANIZATIONS

I have stressed throughout the positive need for commitments by national governments to *ensure* educational equality and to courageous definitions of controversial issues. I do not suggest that all is well in any single country. There are strengths and weaknesses in each country surveyed by the Commission of the European Communities in its 1978 equality project (Byrne, 1979). This is why perhaps the major breakthrough in the 1970s is the growth of the role of the international organizations in bringing together expertise and knowledge of good practice, in publishing research reports and in providing both a forum for development of a clearer consensus, and a lever to persuade regressive governments to become more positively committed to action rather than theory.

At the UN World Congress in Mexico in International Women's Year, a decisive policy statement was approved by 89 votes to 3 by the delegates present, which laid a clear obligation on national governments to realize nine objectives by 1980, two of which are especially relevant here: (a) to *ensure* equality of access to all types and levels of education; and (b) *consciously* to orient school education and adult and continuing education to a revaluation of the role of women and men to *ensure* the 'full flowering of their personalities both within the family and in society'. This matches the directive issued by the Council of the Commission of the European Communities on equal treatment between men and women workers—binding on member states—already quoted. Article 3 of that Directive makes it clear that equal treatment at work has as its prerequisite, *exactly* the same access to all levels and standards of general and technical education, training, advanced training and vocational guidance. It is at least arguable that any differentiation of curricula on grounds of sex is in direct contravention of this directive. What mechanism has the United Kingdom education service for ensuring equal access and identical curriculum, especially in single-sex schools?

In 1977 the European Commission set up its first study on sex inequality at secondary level, completed in 1978, and this now forms the basis of a series of recommendations for a Community action programme to focus on a range of topics identified as of common interest across countries. These are mirrored by a series of current and earlier resolutions and reports from the Council of Europe, the ILO, the European Ministers (the 22). The recommendations centre on four main areas which I suggest might form a backcloth against which to set more detailed discussions.

First, why do girls and boys act and achieve differently in single-sex and coeducational environments? Both the European Commission and the Standing Conference of Ministers recommended that priority be given to research into relative performance in single-sex and mixed schools and this is clearly a highly relevant area. Secondly, the imbalance in the teaching force is worsening all over Europe, with fewer women in leadership in direct proportion to the extension of coeducation and of reorganizations into larger establishments. A strategy is needed to deploy the teaching force more evenly at all levels. Thirdly, the dissemination of the growing and rich pool of new expertise is an increasing problem. How do we distil new ideas, good practice and new evidence on sex differences—and the mythologies to be replaced—to the field worker, the teacher in the classroom, the careers officer in the High Street? Fourthly, there is universal agreement that little progress can be made without major changes to the initial and in-service training of teachers and other workers with young people, and this means a bridge between the expertise in the academic sector, and the practitioners responsible for training and for teaching.

ACTION

Which brings me back to the point of departure—how to move forward on a national plane as well as in the schools and colleges. In Sweden, for example, a report on equality has been sent to all universities and training schools by the Ministry with a request that students and staff and other workers should discuss the new ideas and make proposals. In the Netherlands the Ministry has commissioned a five-year plan from its Emancipation Commission and has already issued some guidelines—and resources—for action. Germany has its positive discrimination programmes. France has established a common curriculum with homecraft for boys and technical education for girls as well as vice versa. The United Kingdom is, so far as I can see, unique in Europe in resolutely abrogating its responsibility to ensure a national system of minimum education which incorporates sex equality, territorial equality, and a common-core curriculum which does not depend on where a child lives, which school it attends, what the philosophy of the current head determines, or what resources the LEA has left after the latest Rate Support Grant Settlement.

Successive governments since 1945 have indeed turned a Nelsonic eye to Section 1 of the Education Act which *requires* the Minister 'to *secure the effective* execution by local authorities under his (her) *control and direction* of the *national policy* for providing a varied and comprehensive educational service in every area' [my italics]. I am not arguing for complete centralization of the detailed system—far from it. But the corollary of total delegation by Ministers to local authorities is the perpetuation of local variations in *basic* rights, not in innovative extras, and an abrogation of Section 1 of the 1944 Act. We need, therefore, still to pursue the question of what schools and colleges can do without waiting for government. But I still hold government ultimately responsible for making sure that it is done— everywhere, and not merely in progressive schools.

According to Goethe 'to act is easy, to think is hard'. I would reverse this maxim—although we should not so lose ourselves in day-to-day work as to lose our capacity for clear thought, neither is debate a substitute for deed. Arnold held that 'If we have the ideas firm and clear the mechanical details for their execution will come a great deal more simply and easily than we now suppose'. I hope that having read this book, readers will agree. And I hope that they will ensure that the Secretary of State also takes the message of his continental colleagues equally to heart. As the Bristol Women's Collective reminded us – 'Women hold up half the sky'. For our destiny, like Malena's, lies out there someplace too.

REFERENCES

Advisory Council on Equality Between Men and Women (1979) *Roles in Transition*, Stockholm, Advisory Council on Equality Between Men and Women.
Auvinen, Riitta (1975). 'Participation of Finnish women in decision-making', in *Research Symposium on Women and Decision-making*, No. 23. Geneva: ILO.
Beture, Département Socio-économique (1974). *Enquête sur la scolarisation au niveau 3ème CAP-BEP dans les arrondissements de Calais, Dunkerque et St Omer*. November 1974. Beture, France.

Byrne, E.M. (1979) *Equality of Education and Training for Girls' Studies*, Education Series No. 9. Commission of the European Communities.

Commission of the European Communities (1975) *Directive on Equality of Treatment Between Men and Women Workers*, 12 February 1975 (COM (75) 36 Final).

Danish Ministry of Education Central Council of Education (1978) U90, *Danish Educational Planning and Policy in a Social Context at the end of the 20th Century*, Danish Ministry of Education.

Délégation à la Condition Féminine (1978). *Attitudes et comportements des parents envers le problème de l'orientation scolaire.* Paris: Délégation à la Condition Féminine.

Gaudart, Dorothea (1975). 'The case of Austria', in *Research Symposium on Women and Decision-making*, No. 23. Geneva: ILO.

Netherlands Second Chamber of the States General (1974–5) *Contours of a Future Education System*, 13–459 (1–2), pp. 89–97.

Nonon, Jacqueline (1978), to the Fifth International Congress of Women Engineers and Scientists, Rouen, 4 September 1978.

Nordic Council for Standing Conference of European Ministers of Education (1979) *Sex Roles and Education*, CME/XI (79)6.

Standing Conference of European Ministers of Education (SCEME) (1979) CME HF (79) 8, June 1979.

United Nations (1967) From Resolution No. 2263 of the General Assembly of the UN, 'Declaration on the elimination of discrimination against women', 7 November 1967. The 1967 text has now been incorporated in the UN's 1979 *Convention on the Elimination of Discrimination Against Women* to which all European countries are signatories.

8

The Schools Council and Gender

a case study in the legitimation of curriculum policy

GABY WEINER

It is now clear that sex differentiation does not *only* affect the option choices made by boys and girls. It affects the relative performance of boys and girls in subjects, such as Mathematics and English Literature, which they continue to take together in large numbers. It affects the relative numbers of boys and girls put in for examinations in such subjects, the level of examination in which they are entered (e.g. CSE or O level), and their examination performance. Pupils who have not shown a sexist bias in their choice of school subjects up to 16 may, nevertheless, revert to tradition in choices they make in the 6th form, in further education and in jobs. The problem is clearly a very complex one (Women's National Commission, *Report on Secondary Education*, WNC, 1983, p 3).[1]

This statement, from a Cabinet Office committee to the government, shows the extent to which gender issues within education have become accepted areas of research and action among educationalists. So much so that 'equal opportunities' is now on many school agendas, and daily, it seems, pronouncements are made by the press concerning the need for more female scientists and technologists.

To understand this interest—and the policies that have flowed from it—it is necessary to look back at earlier initiatives that have helped shape today's thinking. We need to consider the role of anti-discrimination legislation, the work of the Equal Opportunities Commission and the Schools Council, and the pressure from local education authorities and feminist teacher groups. All these elements came together to win the middle-ground in educational ideas and to establish 'gender' as a mainstream educational issue.

Specially commissioned for this volume © 1985 The Open University.

Here I wish to explore the processes which led to the adoption by the
Schools Council, one of the early innovators, of sex differentiation as a
legitimate area of curriculum development and innovation; and then focus in
some detail on the scope and influence of the Schools Council Sex
Differentiation Project (1981–83), which was important despite its minimal
funding and the acknowledged limitations of the Schools Council itself in
effectively implementing curriculum change in schools.

So, how did the Schools Council come to recognize sex-equality as a
necessary part of general curriculum development? The Schools Council for
Curriculum and Examinations established in 1964 'to reappraise syllabuses
and curricula' emerged from a power struggle between the Ministry of
Education, the teacher unions and local authorities over who should control
the curriculum.[2] These three groups, as major members of the Schools
Council, were given the responsibility for curricular and examination reform
although their ability to change existing education practice was always
severely limited. Not only was there little agreement on educational priorities
but they rejected any potential powers of intervention or prescription for
change to school practice.[3] In fact, though the Schools Council was a
centralized agency for curriculum development, it was firmly committed to
pluralism and the support of teachers' professional autonomy.[4]

Acknowledging its self-imposed limitations, the Council's main strategy
for curriculum reform remained the same throughout its lifetime; it
sponsored curriculum development projects, almost 180 in all. During its first
phase (1964–78) these tended to be large in scale and national in scope. After
its reorganization in 1978, the projects were almost all low-financed (*viz.* Sex
Differentiation Project's allocation of £15,000 over 2 years) and often local.

In a perceptive analysis of the Council's work, Raggatt shows that, given
the different interests of Council members, no particular line of curriculum
development could ever be endorsed. Instead projects were sponsored
individually, although post-1978 they were grouped under themes. Furthermore there was always controversy about how effective the Council was in
publicizing its activities and how well it promoted project material.[5] This had
considerable implications for the design and structure of the Sex Differentiation Project.

Despite its divided membership and its considerable internal problems, the
Schools Council was the first national educational body to make a formal
commitment to addressing the issue of sex-differentiation in schooling.
Prior to this, the Council's only engagement in equal opportunities had
been in its controversial and unpublished venture into race relations in
teaching.

What, then, were the reasons for its entry into a similarly highly sensitive
curriculum area? There were a number of factors which caused pressure on
the Council to adopt gender as an educational issue. The first was a draft
resolution from the EEC in 1979 'concerning measures to be taken in the

field of education to improve the preparation of girls for working life and to promote equality of opportunities for girls and boys in society'.[6]

The Council responded by stating that it 'is anxious to make what contribution it can to the development of basic curricula, teaching materials and programmes of career education, which eliminate sex-stereotyping and promote equality of opportunities between the sexes'.[7] This formal policy statement provided the necessary justification and impetus for future work undertaken by the Council in this area.

At the same time the members of some of the Schools Council's curriculum committees, particularly the Secondary Committee, began to argue both for the higher prioritization of equal opportunities issues, and for educational sex differentiation to be addressed more directly. Alongside these, officers within the Council expressed their own interest. Lesley Kant, a principal officer within the Examinations Teams, was particularly active in facilitating a wider discussion of gender issues within the Council.

As if to further prod the Council into action, the Equal Opportunities Commission (EOC) approached the Council's secretary, John Mann, to see if any cooperative work could be undertaken between the two bodies. A meeting between Schools Council and EOC officers resulted in a jointly published series of anti-sexist resource books.[8]

In Autumn 1979 an item concerning sex differentiation first appeared on the agenda of the Secondary Curriculum Committee. Lesley Kant, for the committee, drew the attention of the members to the earlier Council equal opportunities initiatives and recommended the establishment of a subcommittee. This, she claimed, would investigate the extent of sex differentiation in schools and draw up guidelines of good practice. Her arguments were accepted, and the Schools Council Sex Differentiation in School Working Party (quickly renamed SIDESWIPE) was established, drawing its membership from a wide range of interest groups from within the Schools Council (including the teacher unions and Her Majesty's Inspectorate) and from outside bodies such as the Careers' Service and the Industrial Training Boards.

Once established, SIDESWIPE was quickly able to exert influence over Schools Council policy through the political adroitness of its chair, Jack Chambers (later to become president of the National Union of Teachers) and Lesley Kant, who guided the political and administrative decisions of the working party, wrote position papers and conducted extensive 'in house' education.

When, late in 1979, the Council was reorganizing its work by moving away from its former large project structure to four programmes of work, each with a range of activities grouped broadly round a particular theme, SIDESWIPE lobbied for some work on gender to be included within Programme 3, *Curriculum for a Changing World*.[9]

Two particular issues emerged as relevant to the focus of SIDESWIPE.

First, the male domination of scientific and technological subjects at secondary level which had already received some airing as a result of the EOC/SSRC project, *Girls into Science and Technology* (1979–83), and secondly, the more general need to raise awareness of the existence of sex differentiation within schools and thereby reduce it.

This second issue was embraced by *Schools Council Sex Differentiation Project* which had as its brief 'to seek ways of reducing sex-role differentiation in the curriculum...by reviewing and developing existing work on sex differentiation and disseminating examples of "good" or "interesting" practice'.[10] It is this activity which I shall now consider in some detail because of its broad remit and also because its structure and style of work drew on curriculum development strategies pioneered by the Council.

THE SCHOOLS COUNCIL SEX DIFFERENTIATION PROJECT—FROM THE INSIDE

There was some discussion at the beginning of the project as to whether better use would be made of the money allocated to this activity (£15,000 over two years) by sharing it out between individual local authorities. Eventually it was decided that the appointment of a worker was essential in order to exploit fully the existence of the activity within the Council.

Furnished with only the most general guidance about how to organize the work of the project, I was appointed to the post of part-time project coordinator in February 1981. SIDESWIPE was designated the project's steering group and Lesley Kant was appointed its lead officer.[11]

The project was divided into three main areas of work. The most important was that of initiating, supporting and developing teacher group work in a number of local authorities. The second was the accumulation of examples of current practice in the area of sex differentiation in education, both to inform teachers working with the project and others who might be interested in undertaking work in this area.

Funding was insufficient to deal with this aspect of project work, so a successful application was made to the EOC for extra funds to establish an Equal Opportunities Resource Centre at the Schools Council.[12] This supplemented the work of the project at no extra cost to the Council. Hence, by the end of the two-year project, a resource bank made up of existing and newly developed material was available and readily accessible to teachers.[13]

Finally, a newsletter series of four issues was planned for the early dissemination of the work of the project (dissemination was a key feature of all Schools Council projects of the time), to encourage discussion of issues of gender and schooling as widely as possible and to establish a network of people interested in similar aspects of the project's work.

An indication that the project was meeting a general requirement for

Table 1
Activity: *Sex Differentiation*

Current status	Collaboration with SC Working Party on Sex Differentiation in Schools
Timetable	Outline article inviting responses from those interested in setting up teacher groups prepared for next issue of SC Newsletter (autumn 1980). P/T co-ordinator to be appointed end 1980.
Pattern of work	P/T seconded co-ordinator, teacher centre based, responsible for establishment and support of teacher groups—provision of some guidance and information materials, facilitating interchange of ideas between groups, in-service education.
Expected outcomes	Attitude change revealed through school curriculum development and production of specific school curriculum materials. Also video tapes of work in action and co-ordinator's report on good practice.
Dissemination strategy	Teacher groups to provide a platform for future development work. Schools Council production of curriculum materials in published form and co-ordinator's report for possible publication and publicity.
Geographical distribution	Dependent on LEA and newsletter responses. Preferably primary focus and North of England where need is arguably greatest.

Source: Paper 1, Programme 3 Monitoring and Review Group (29.4.1980), The Schools Council.

information on gender and education was given when the newsletter series became very popular, especially when the four national newsletters were supplemented by two focusing specifically on the wide range of ILEA initiatives. The newsletters were reprinted several times and the project mailing list became one of the largest of all Schools Council projects.[14]

PROJECT METHODOLOGY

In considering the way the project was organized, it is important to recognize the limitations of the Schools Council mentioned earlier in this paper. It had no power to decide who would be involved in the project—it was left to local authorities to opt in (or out) and to select the teachers that would participate, although the status the Council enjoyed among some local authorities meant that teachers were able to be released, for example, for day conferences or to get to after school meetings.

This meant, to some extent, that those teachers (and LEAs) who became involved with the project were already committed and enthusiastic. They therefore saw the main thrust of the project as that of raising awareness among their colleagues. They argued that whilst many of their colleagues appeared to have a professional commitment to equality of opportunity, they dismissed discussion of gender by denying the existence of sex differentiation in their school—'We in this school treat boys and girls in exactly the same way', was an oft quoted response.

Project teachers therefore defined the principal aim of teacher group work as that of *awareness-raising*; of persuading teachers with little or no awareness that *sexism in schools is an educational problem.*

In order to do this, they first considered those specific elements of school life which were most likely to influence the perceptions and performance of pupils and then find out, through in-depth studies, the extent of sex differentiation in their schools. These studies were then written up and presented at staff meetings and to local authority personnel as a basis for general discussion among colleagues.

The following topics emerged as suitable candidates for closer analysis, covering areas of the overt and hidden school curriculum.

(a) *Sex differentiation in whole school areas*—gathering information on option choice, examination entry and results as a preliminary for more focused work.

(b) *Sex bias in reading schemes, textbooks and teaching resources*—analysing curricular material for stereotyping and irrelevance to pupils' lives.

(c) *Sex bias in specific subjects or departmental areas*—examining the 'milieu' of a subject or department, for instance, by analysing staffing patterns, examination entry and results, pupil attitudes, option choice, to gain a clear overview of the working of a department.

(d) *The 'hidden' curriculum*—looking at implicit as well as formal aspects of the curriculum, e.g. assemblies, uniform, out-of-school activities, teacher and pupil attitude and expectation.

(e) *Classroom relationships*—considering by observation and monitoring the relationship between pupils in the classroom and between pupils and teachers.

(f) *Careers education*—examining the effects of the content and timing of careers advice.

(g) *Language use in school*-undertaking studies of language use in all areas of school life, e.g. within the classroom, in the playground, in school booklets and parent publications.

(h) *The changing curriculum*—looking at changes in the school curriculum brought about by the decline of traditional forms of employment and the growth of computer technology.

In summarizing the work of the project, and particularly in seeking an explanation for why changes of practice were successfully implemented in certain cases and not in others, two important features were identified;

Awareness raising. This is the means by which the issues of sex-differentiation and stereotyping are raised, for instance, in informal staff discussion, at staff conferences and parents' evenings. The aims are to persuade teachers and parents of the importance of change and to promote awareness and information about the issues.

Institutional support. This is the method by which official sanctions are given to encourage teachers to change their practice in a particular way. Approval may be given, say, through promotion or allocation of resources.[16]

Awareness without institutional support, it was claimed, might mean initial enthusiasm without sufficient resources for implementation, whereas institutional support without awareness, e.g. LEA policy commitment with insufficient in-service provision, was likely to result in superficial rather than serious commitment to change.

THE SCHOOLS COUNCIL AND GENDER

The principal approach of the Schools Council to the work of the Sex Differentiation Project and to its other initiatives on gender was that teachers differentiated between pupils either because they were ignorant about the implications of their practice or because they were ill-informed about what could be termed women's (or feminist) issues.

For the Council, therefore, the solution to problems of sex differentiation and discrimination lay primarily with educators—it therefore recommended educational remedies of improving the professionalism and pedagogy of teachers. It was anticipated that attempts at consciousness-raising and an emphasis on pedagogical improvement would lead teachers to adopt, voluntarily, anti-sexist professional practices.

In some ways, the Sex Differentiation Project provided the Council with evidence that there was some substance to its faith in voluntary professional change. The newsletters and a contact mailing list generated a considerable number of conferences, publications and in-service courses on developing anti-sexist classroom strategies and an increasing number of local education authorities and schools created their own equal opportunities policies.

Furthermore, it was evident that the project had a broader base of support than had first been envisaged—on the announcement of the closure of the Schools Council by Keith Joseph, in 1982, Joan Lestor, for the Opposition, cited the extension of the work of the Sex Differentiation Project as a reason for the Council's continued existence.[17] More difficult to gauge is its impact on general classroom practice, despite the focus of the teacher groups on developing strategies immediately applicable to the classroom.

One suspects that this project suffered from many of the inadequacies of other Schools Council projects and that its effects, in all but a few classrooms, were marginal in changing the attitudes and perception of the average school teacher.[18]

IMPLICATIONS FOR GENERAL POLICYMAKING

Does the experience of the Schools Council's initiatives on gender have any implications for general curriculum policy-making? I suggest that there are several.

First, the fact that the Schools Council enjoyed relatively high status at head teacher and LEA level ensured that its acceptance of sex differentiation as a legitimate area for the professional development of teachers was widely noted and endorsed. This made it easier for resources to be allocated at national and local levels.

Secondly, by using the national network already established by the Council, it was possible for ideas on gender to be discussed more widely. For example, the newsletter series was sent to every LEA, higher education institution and teachers' centre as well as to those who had already indicated their interest.

Thirdly, because the project was based at the Council and drew on strategies for curriculum change pioneered by the Schools Council, its work found acceptance with another important group, with curriculum developers, researchers and academics within and outside the Council. It therefore extended discussion of gender issues yet further.

Finally, the importance of having committed individuals in senior positions in educational institutions was sharply illuminated by the political role that Lesley Kant, principal officer in the Examination team, played in establishing the Sex Differentiation in Schools Working Party (SIDE-SWIPE) and in alerting officers within the Council to possibilities for future and sustained action.

One view of the Schools Council's work on gender is that it achieved some of the tasks it set itself. It raised general awareness and it produced examples of anti-sexist practice—however, due to its closure, which only the most pessimistic predicted, its national work on sex differentiation began and ended with the Sex Differentiation Project. Without resources, institutional support, access to national networks of contacts and people in high places, an important area of curriculum innovation and development has been sharply curtailed.

The Schools Council was effective because it provided resources and an institutional framework which persuaded teachers that the educational establishment thought eradicating sex differentiation and sexual bias from their schools was an aim worth striving for. Who will give them those cues now?

NOTES AND REFERENCES

1. Women's National Commission, *Report on Secondary Education*, WNC, London, 1983.
2. Department of Education and Science, *Aspects of Secondary Education in England*, HMSO, London, 1966.
3. Salter, B. and Tapper, B., *Education, Politics and the State: the theory and practice of educational change*, Grant McIntyre, London, 1981.
4. Caston, G., The Schools Council in context, *Journal of Curriculum Studies*, Vol. 3, No. 1, May 1971, pp. 50–64.
5. Raggatt, P., Agencies of change, Unit 27 of *Purposes and Planning in the Curriculum* (E204), Open University Press, Milton Keynes, 1983.
6. Schools Council Internal Report, Annex A SC 79/297, 1979.
7. Schools Council Internal Report, Annex C SC 79/297, 1979.
8. Four booklets were produced in all:
Eddowes, M., *Humble-pi: the Mathematics Education of Girls*, 1983.
Harding, J., *Switched Off: the Science Education of Girls*, 1983.
Stones, R., *'Pour out the Cocoa, Janet': Sexism in Children's Books*, 1983
Whyte, J., *Beyond the Wendy House: Sex Role Stereotyping in Primary Schools*, 1983.
All published by Longmans, Harlow, for the Schools Council.
9. The other Programmes of work were Programme 1, *Purpose and Planning in Schools*, Programme 2, *Helping Individual Teachers Become More Effective*, and Programme 4, *Individual Pupils*.
10. Schools Council Internal Report (1980) Programme 3, *Monitoring and Review Group*, 29 April 1980.
11. Due to the Grant awarded by the EOC (see note 12), I was joined by a part-time seconded teacher who was appointed to set up a resource centre; and the project team was further supplemented by a one-year secondment from ILEA.
12. The application was made in the name of Lesley Kant and Gaby Weiner as the EOC awards grants to individuals rather than the institutions.
13. Since the closure of the Schools Council, the Equal Opportunities Resource Centre has been lodged at the Schools Curriculum Development Council (SCDC).
14. Millman, V. and Weiner, G., *Sex Differentiation in Schooling: Is there really a problem?* Longman, Harlow, 1985.
15. Op. cit.
16. Op. cit.
17. Hansard, 1982, *Oral Answers*, 9 November 1982, HMSO, London.
18. Steadman, S., Pearson, C. and Salter, B., *The Impact and Take Up Project*, Schools Council, London, 1982.

9

A Local Authority Initiative on Equal Opportunities

HAZEL TAYLOR

A local education authority which decides that it places a high priority on gender equality and wishes to develop an initiative to implement equal opportunities is faced with various questions in determining how to go about such a process. In an outer London borough, which I shall call *Rickley*, an initial decision to appoint an adviser in the education department to lead such an initiative led to subsequent decisions on methods and range of implementation. Several factors were of crucial importance in determining the success (or otherwise) of the effort, and these will be considered in the course of a mainly descriptive account of what has happened. These factors can be briefly summarized.

Firstly, the relationship between the political instigation of the policy and the need for it to be seen as a professional issue by schools is a delicate one, and has to be handled with great awareness of the sensitivities of many teachers.

Secondly, there has to be full consideration of the factors which must impede change within the education service, with a recognition that structural change and change within individual classrooms have different effects.

Thirdly, there are differences between different types of school in the ways in which power is distributed and an analysis of this will lead to differences of approach by the authority.

Fourthly, the relationships between the authority and its schools can be mobilized to bring about change, if the authority chooses: the provision of resources, the use of the advisory service and in-service training and so on, are all available for redistribution in accordance with the authority's priorities.

Specially commissioned for this volume © 1985 The Open University.

Perhaps the most important factor in the whole discussion is recognition of the stages which must be gone through for change to be effective; no one of these stages, which different people will go through at different times, can be omitted. There must be an initial stage of growing awareness, time for the subsiding of fears, time to become properly informed, time to work on change.

Finally, after all the initial work in preparing the ground for change has been done, the effects of changes must be monitored, those involved must be supported and effects evaluated continually.

Concern among some educationalists for gender equality in education began to emerge in the mid-seventies, with the setting up of the Equal Opportunities Commission and the publication of such books as Eileen Byrne's *Women and Education* (1978) and the DES survey *Curricular Differences for Boys and Girls* (1975). This concern was further expressed within Spender and Sarah's *Learning to Lose* (1980), which showed that feminist teachers were working within schools to take steps to achieve change. At the same time, attempts to achieve racial equality were under way in several local education authorities, and debate in some local labour parties in particular began to focus on ways of developing initiatives which would deal with gender as well. In *Rickley* such a discussion produced the suggestion, from women party members, that appointing an adviser for equal opportunities within the education department would be an effective way of mounting and implementing an initiative. This idea was taken up by the Labour group on the council, who were in control, and plans went ahead in mid-1981 to recruit to the post, which would be the first such post in the country. There was by no means widespread support for this move, for a variety of reasons. It was opposed by the teachers' unions within the borough, NALGO, the Chief Education Officer, and the Conservative opposition on the council. The Conservative opposition was straightforward and took the form of complete rejection of any need for a gender equality initiative. It branded the idea of an adviser as yet another example of the money wasting of the extreme left. The opposition from other sources came from a mixture of belief that such a post was not indeed necessary, and concern that a new post should be established when cuts were being made in other parts of the education service. The teachers' unions in particular were against a post which might be paid for by cuts in teacher numbers. A job description was nevertheless drawn up, and an appointment was offered at a point two months before the local government elections of May 1982. The Labour Party were by no means sure of retaining control of the council, and at the interviews for the post the Conservative education spokesman told all candidates that if the Conservatives won the election they would immediately disestablish the post. Labour responded by offering the selected candidate a guaranteed minimum contract of two years; Conservatives replied by claiming that if they couldn't make the postholder redundant, she would be redeployed. At the election, Labour retained control on the strength of the Mayor's casting vote; the equal opportunities adviser took up her post twenty-six days later.

It is impossible to discuss the implementation of this initiative without knowing of this political background; party political decisions were central in creating the post, and the manifesto of the Labour Party at the 1982 election contained a clear commitment to the issue of gender equality. The adviser, once in post, was initially closely identified with a political initiative, and was received according to people's views about the local Labour administration. While she had a clear mandate from the council, she did not have support, or even informed neutrality, within the education department, and had a notoriety in schools before she arrived. Her responsibilities were to 'eliminate sex stereotyping' across the entire education service, from under 5s to further education, with the status and general duties of other advisers, and access to the same ways of working as any local authority inspector/adviser: in-service training, school visiting, the power to give advice and make recommendations, and to use such resources as the Education Committee allocated for her work.

It might be expected that, once the appointment had been made, discussions would have taken place between the adviser and senior officers about the issues of equal opportunities, and about strategies to be developed to implement the manifesto commitment. In fact, this did not happen, and the strategies for implementation were, after one meeting with members, left to her to devise. In December 1983 Labour lost overall control of the council and Conservatives became committee chairs, with Liberal support. The equal opportunities initiatives are still council policy, because of the Liberal support of the Labour stand on this issue; but there is far less active political pressure for their implementation than there was before the change of control.

PROFESSIONALIZING THE ISSUE

In devising and implementing an initiative, the main concern was to establish provision of and access to equal opportunities regardless of gender or race, as a central issue which is fundamental to education for a democratic society. A major initiative to develop multicultural education with an anti-racist perspective was already under way within the authority.

It was important to make clear that equality of opportunity was a concept well accepted within education; new ways of looking at what happened within existing systems and new evidence about the outcomes of schooling demonstrated that gender equality, like race equality, was not being achieved. The task for teachers therefore was to take on board that evidence, and develop changes in practice to bring about the desired outcome. That outcome would be seen as desirable by the vast majority of educators, not simply those in sympathy with the particular ideologies of the politicians who proposed the initiative: though it must not be forgotten that, without those politicians, the initiative would never have been implemented to anything like the extent to which it has been.

The requirement by the Education Committee and council for action on equal opportunities has been a central factor in producing change. The two sides cannot be separated—on the one hand, change to provide equality is good practice; on the other hand, change is necessary because the council says so. Either without the other would not succeed: the former because it would not apply widely enough to have an overall effect, the latter because it would lead to token change without commitment or understanding. This sounds very simple—some would say simplistic—and at heart it is. The complications arise not in the acceptance of the need, but in debates about the causes, about the methods to be used to change, about the exact nature of the outcomes to be aimed for. Not least of the problems lies in dealing with those teachers who believe that the rightness of equality of opportunity is so self-evident that they must be providing it; others lie with the difficulties of any innovation: intellectual acceptance of the need, but enormous forces of subconscious fear, inertia, the essential conservatism of schools as institutions, excess workload, lack of resources. All these have to be taken into consideration in planning strategies.

CHOOSING THE CHANGE AGENTS

The identification of gender equality as a democratic right carries immediate implications for implementation, which again had to be considered when planning strategies. If the issue is fundamentally concerned with the power sharing aspects of democracy, to what extent must policy be democratically produced, and by whom? A top-down model of change is clearly not appropriate (even if it would be effective); a bottom-up model is harder to support and likely to produce divergence between institutions, but is the model philosophically most acceptable to the nature of the initiative. It is also morally and practically desirable, as it forces acknowledgement of the fact that much of the innovative work, both in defining the problems in providing an education for gender equality, and in developing practice to bring it about, has been and is actually being done by teachers within their schools. A bottom-up approach also acknowledges that in this area what happens within individual classrooms is often of greater consequence than the structures of the institution, which are the areas which top-down change addresses first. The method of approach, therefore, was one of fostering and supporting bottom-up change, and one means of enabling that was to secure top-down support and co-operation. It followed that policy-making should be carried out at the level of individual institutions, with an overall enabling policy statement from the council to mandate the work.

The thinking about the issue outlined above led to a number of concurrent steps to implement the initiative. An initial report to the Education Committee, within two months of the adviser's appointment, contained the following policy statement, which was adopted by the full council:

> The Council of the London Borough of *Rickley*, responsible for the education of girls and boys in a population of 250,000, believes that girls and boys, women and men, are inherently equal but acknowledges that there are many ways in which women and girls are at present discriminated against and rendered unequal;
>
> recognises that the present inequality of opportunity and achievement in girls and boys is in part due to those school practices which unconsciously differentiate between girls and boys, and recognises that to provide equality of opportunity for both sexes involves far more than the mere equal availability of subject choices for girls and boys;
>
> commits itself to the elimination of school practices which discriminate between girls and boys through an examination by schools of curriculum content and organisational methods, and to sustained development of non-sexist practices;
>
> commits itself to a continuous monitoring of the progress made in providing non-sexist education as an integral part of the school experience of all pupils.

STAGES OF WORKING

At the same time, the adviser began her task of establishing the central educational importance of the issue, of securing top level support, and of fostering bottom-up change. This was done in a variety of ways: by meeting as many teachers as possible, by bringing together groups who shared an existing interest in equal opportunities, and by running a variety of in-service training courses. The whole of the first year of implementation was spent in planning long term measures, identifying and linking allies, and creating a favourable climate of opinion for discussion of the issues and openness to change. The importance of making personal contacts was considerable, and the authority was small enough to make it feasible for one person to visit a large proportion of the schools. The personal contacts meant that the issue of equal opportunities could be identified with a person who was clearly an ordinary adviser with a solid professional background, not a naive agent of the easily stereotyped politicians behind the initiative. They also were the beginning step in creating personal commitment and involvement. Visiting head teachers in particular was a means of discussing their difficulties in educating children for the modern world, and indicating a sensible awareness of the constraints upon them. This development of personal commitment to an issue is important, too, in an area of change where personal attitudes play a large part in the effectiveness of implementation of change strategies. With an issue like secondary reorganization, personal attitudes, though relevant, can be disregarded as major physical and administrative changes require co-operation from teachers or cause them considerable discomfiture. Lack of co-operation from individuals in equal opportunities measures means at best no change, and at worst the undermining of those colleagues who are trying to implement them.

The programme of visits to schools ran parallel to a series of meetings set up to bring together people who expressed an interest in the issue. It was the case that a great deal of work had been done in a few schools before the adviser's arrival, and that the teaching force in general within the authority was probably more open to new ideas than many, having already taken some steps to come to terms with the demands of racial equality. There were therefore many teachers who were concerned about gender equality and anxious to be involved in measures to create it. One of the reasons for a central authority policy statement was to give authority validation to the work of those teachers. One general forum was already in existence, an equal opportunities panel at the Teachers' Centre, which met regularly; and it was they who organized a welcome meeting for the adviser. Subsequently, several further groups formed, initially focusing on the need to develop class-room materials which avoided the problems of stereotyping, under-representation of women, he/man language and so on of most commercial material.

FITTING THE APPROACH TO THE INSTITUTION

The adviser's brief clearly encompassed the entire service and one question which had to be considered was whether exactly the same methods of implementation were appropriate for both primary and secondary schools. Bottom-up change might be easier to achieve in secondary schools, where there was a sizeable number of committed teachers across all departments who could form a working party and act as a catalyst within the staff. In primary schools it was unlikely that the staff would be large enough for a working party to be an effective change agent: on a small staff it could be seen as divisive, and a small working party could easily be marginalized. There are also key differences in the delegation of the head teacher's power in the two sectors of education. The support of the secondary head teacher as an individual is very important to the implementation of equal opportunities but his or her active involvement in that is not necessarily essential, as delegated power for curriculum and pastoral organization lies with other members of the senior management, and one of them is perhaps the key figure. The primary head teacher, with a very much smaller organization, keeps far greater personal control over the development of curriculum and organiza-tional changes and is likely either to be the leader in any initiative, or to be an essential enabler. The direct involvement of primary head teachers in equal opportunities initiatives was therefore seen as crucial to their implementation in primary schools, while in secondary schools a named member of the senior staff was needed. There were two other areas of difference between the two phases which were seen as important: one was the difference in the perception of the relevance of the issue, and related to that was the difference in the amount of published research and other documentation of the issue as it related to each phase. The general perception of the provision of equal opportunities as an educational issue relates to the provision of all curriculum areas for all pupils in secondary schools, and to the differential take-up of subjects along fairly clear sex-typed lines at option choice time. HMI interest and research has concentrated on the performance and aspirations of girls and boys in secondary schools, and it has apparently been assumed that the issue had little relevance for the primary school. There have been few studies of gender difference in primary schools—Clarricoates (1980) and Delamont (1980) have been lone voices amongst sociologists of education. However, it is the case that, in general, primary education lays foundations which are built on later and that it would be extremely strange, to say the least, if gender differences were unique amongst features of child development in springing up fully fledged in a child at adolescence. The adviser decided that an effective programme for implementing gender equality had to begin at the beginning, which in educational terms was with the nursery school or class, and build from there positive attitudes to and expectations of gender equality. She therefore developed her work so that initially (in the first three years) more time and resources were spent on implementation in the primary sector than the secondary, though the secondary sector was not ignored.

PATTERNS OF CHANGE IMPLEMENTATION IN SECONDARY SCHOOLS

What emerged from consideration of all the factors mentioned above was a report to the Education Committee called 'Equal Opportunities in the Primary School: an action programme', which made a number of recommendations for implementing the initiative in primary schools. No similar report has yet been done for secondary schools, although it is likely that it will be by the summer of 1985. The secondary schools have been allowed the freedom to develop strategies for gender equality without the framework of council requirements beyond the overall policy commitment, and the pace and quality of change varies from school to school. This is inevitable given the differences between schools, and must be allowed to be so. If an authority is concerned with the quality of the developments within its schools, then it must recognize that they cannot all start from different points and arrive at the finishing post at the same time; at the same time there must be enough in the way of requirements and inducements to ensure that all of the schools are actually on the course, going in the same direction. In most secondary schools, the pattern of effort takes the form of establishing an equal opportunities working party, with a requirement to report back to the head teacher via the channels normally operating within the school. There are working parties in thirteen of the authority's eighteen high schools, including both of the boys' schools and one of the two girls' schools. In three other schools, equal opportunities is included in the terms of reference of a Curriculum Review Committee. These working parties are, at varying paces, and with varying degrees of support from other staff, examining their schools and making recommendations for change. In some schools, major changes have been effected in organization and curriculum, and the point has been reached where a detailed whole school policy has been prepared, discussed and accepted by the whole staff. In others, minor changes are being made and the pace is very slow. This is usually due to two factors: the number of active people in the working party, and a tradition of slow response to change in the school. It is really not surprising that schools with a tradition of democratic staff involvement in and desire for educationally desirable development have responded more quickly to the equal opportunities initiative than those where the style is different.

Most of the working parties were set up after an initial three-day course for key members of management teams, which was attended by heads or deputies from all of the secondary schools and which was addressed by the Director of Education. The aim of the course was to establish the areas of concern and bring about a commitment to change. In order to monitor what was happening in the secondary schools, and to provide some support and input of new ideas, two termly meetings are held, one of the members of the original course, and one of representatives of the Equal Opportunities Working Parties. There is some overlap of membership of the two groups, but the focus of meeting for each is quite different. The first group comes together to discuss management of change, while the second meeting is a forum for issues of common concern between schools, such as balance of women and men teachers, or sexual harassment. At the same time, examination results are analysed by gender each year, and provide evidence of the success—or lack of it—in changing patterns of option choice. The provision of in-service courses on various aspects of gender equality provision, and work by and with specialist subject advisers, continually increases the number of people who understand the importance of the issue, and the ways in which discrimination takes place. As they go back to their schools, it becomes easier for the working party to make progress.

As has already been said, plans for implementing the authority's initiative in primary schools were laid down by the authority in a much more detailed way than for the secondary schools, and most of the steps in the initial report to the Education Committee have now been taken.

EFFECTIVE CHANGE REQUIRES EFFECTIVE MANAGERS

It has been suggested earlier in the chapter that the implementation of equal opportunities initiatives cannot be divorced from an appreciation of the effectiveness of a school's management; a desire to change that is not supported by effective management techniques to bring change about is no more satisfactory than no intention of changing, and can produce an extremely frustrating atmosphere for young teachers to work in. Sometimes the sheer inadequacy of management can appear to be a refusal to put into practice the desire expressed in words to make changes, and seem like a complicated indirect subversion of the policy initiative. Given the vast variation in management effectiveness, and in levels of knowledge and commitment amongst the authority's primary head teachers, it seemed sensible to combine five elements in the primary action programme. Firstly, it was clearly necessary to provide information to indicate that an equal opportunities initiative was essential. Secondly, it was also essential to allow time for that knowledge to sink in and increase and spread, helped in various ways by additional input. Thirdly, it was essential to be as helpful as possible about how the changes which were deemed necessary could be brought about, without impinging too much on head teachers' autonomy but recognizing the many pressures they are under. Fourthly, it was essential to make resources available, and fifthly, to work with classroom teachers as well as head teachers at the same time, so that there was a two-way fertilization process going on in the schools. The implementation programme hopefully took all five elements into account.

THE PRIMARY INITIATIVE

The report to the Education Committee reviewed the need for an equal opportunities initiative to be taken seriously in primary schools. It was a longer-than-usual report, and provided quite detailed information, initially for committee members. It also outlined recommendations for action. At the request of councillors a slightly longer version was prepared called *Really Equal?*, in more everyday language, and with an attractive cover, which was then placed on the agenda of all governing bodies. It thus became an initial discussion document in all schools. The length and the language of the document were crucial factors in its generally favourable reception. It was long enough to give a range of examples of its points, and to cover all the main areas of concern: so that the issue could not be trivialized by inviting a very low level of response. There is evidence from other authorities that initial policy statements or guidelines on equal opportunities that are oversimplified do produce some very ill-considered responses; this was avoided, as the document took a serious tone and demanded a reasoned response. The everyday language was also crucial because the serious points were made in terms that governors and teachers could easily understand and without arousing the suspicion and hostility that sociological jargon or committee language rightly produces in those it mystifies. Responses to the document came back via the committee clerks to the adviser so that she knew what head teachers were saying to their governing bodies; the issue was firmly on the agenda for primary schools, and primary heads and staff knew that they had to do something about it. The document recommended courses for head teachers, a range of other in-service training courses, including some for non-teaching staff, a working party to provide guidelines for good practice in primary schools, and for four schools to be designated to carry out action research in areas where there was insufficient evidence of what happens in primary schools—such as in interaction in the classroom and gender, well documented now for secondary schools but largely ignored in primary. It also recommended that all schools should produce a whole school policy on equal opportunities by the end of the school year following the discussion of the initial document—i.e. nearly two years later. This timescale was chosen because of the need for knowledge of the issues and how to do something about them to be built up; it was felt that the preparation of policy statements by staff that were not well informed would actually delay or prevent institutionalization of effective change strategies.

Even with this time-scale, there are schools where meaningless policy is being prepared; there are, however, far fewer of those than there would have been without the two-year preparation time.

All the primary head teachers were then invited to a three-day course, to present the issues in greater depth, to provide discussion time, and to disseminate strategies for change. The course which was planned with a group of head teachers was run four times over a year, and was attended by nearly all the head teachers. The heads of Church of England schools were those most likely not to attend. Heads who did not attend a final course specially arranged for those who did not attend earlier courses, and who did not send their apologies in writing to the primary adviser, received a letter from the Director of Education noting their non-attendance. The presence of this letter on file usually secured co-operation. There are important issues here concerning the implementation of a policy initiative, the autonomy of head teachers and a belief in the importance of schools' control over policy-making. The view was taken that if the authority, on the decision of its members, takes up a major policy initiative, then the responsibility for its implementation rests with every teacher within the authority, and that if governing bodies, with their responsibility for the oversight of the curriculum and management of schools, delegate to head teachers the authority to implement agreed policy, then it is the duty of head teachers to do so. If in-service training to enable them to do this is provided in school time, and at the authority's expense, and if they are allowed considerable freedom in the exact content of the policy, then it is reasonable to expect them to attend. The position in relation to voluntary aided or controlled schools is of course different, and it was found that head teachers of the Catholic schools were more prepared to co-operate with the authority than were the Anglican or the Jewish ones.

While the head teachers' courses were being held, a working party of primary teachers was meeting on a monthly basis to formulate recommendations and guidelines for good practice to provide equal opportunities. The working party's members were teachers nominated by schools and were a wide cross-section of teachers, mostly on Scale 1 or 2. The working party met for just over a year, with additional meetings in its last six months; the members were released from their schools for one afternoon a month and other meetings were held in their own time.

The report is, at the time of writing this article, in its first draft and out for consultation to various groups within the borough. A copy of it will go to every primary teacher. It will be available to stimulate a second stage of discussion in schools before the policies are finally prepared, and to provide ideas for implementation of various points likely to be recommended in the policy statements.

Action research projects are being carried out in four schools: to discover ways of introducing technology into the primary curriculum whilst creating confidence and positive attitudes in girls towards it, and science; to develop methods of increasing girls' confidence in mathematics; to document and review the nature of the pupil–pupil and pupil–teacher interaction in junior classes, and to develop ways of working with parents in the provision of equal opportunities for girls and boys. These projects will provide material to be disseminated to other schools in the authority and the status of the research will lend further credibility to the issues. The range of in-service training for primary teachers has included a part theory, part practical fifteen afternoons course, a three-day 'Running a non-sexist classroom' course, repeated in ten evening sessions, a number of courses on stereotyping in books, and workshop sessions on making materials.

Head teachers were subsequently reminded of the need to produce a policy statement, and a further half day meeting was arranged for them at which they shared with each other the steps already taken in their schools, and discussed ways of involving the whole staff in the preparation of a meaningful policy. The attendance at the meetings was high, and the range of practice described was very wide. It was clear that in many schools much had already been done, while in others the issue was still, in spite of the authority's efforts, not being taken with sufficient seriousness. The feedback from heads was very positive, as they valued sharing and learning from each other. It was strongly recommended that the policy should take the form of an agreed set of aims for the school, and a series of objectives to be implemented by an agreed time to achieve the aims. It was accepted that some objectives would

take much longer than others to achieve, and that some, such as the rewriting
and resourcing of topic areas to reflect the values of gender and race equality,
would require the allocation of a proportion of capitation over a period of
years.

These policy statements are now in preparation.

As depth of understanding of the issue has grown, so has demand for
support and resources. The adviser has had a little 'pump-priming' money for
curriculum development, and specifically for non-sexist books, but it is felt
that as the changes needed are central they should be funded by schools as
they would fund other developments, from capitation. The authority is not
one in which years of cuts have greatly reduced capitation levels. The need
for support for curriculum development work is great, and two primary and
two secondary teachers have been seconded for two years as part of a rolling
programme to the authority's Curriculum Development Support Unit to
work on non-sexist classroom materials with groups of teachers, and to
provide other forms of support in schools.

INTERIM EVALUATION

The initiative is now in an interim stage of implementation, and it is
possible to make some initial comments about what is taking place. There is
clear evidence that overall the level of knowledge about and the development
of positive attitudes to gender equality is for more widespread than in other
authorities, and is a matter of remark by teachers who move to other
authorities or go on out-borough courses. Real change does not necessarily
follow from increased knowledge and awareness, however, and it is too early
to say how widespread that will be, or how swift. In many schools, easy
changes have taken place, many of which do institutionalize the principle of
gender equality. Integrated registers, lists, lines, assembly seating and games
do reverse the hidden message of gender difference of the previous separated
arrangements. In a few schools there have been breakthroughs into
curriculum revision, and there is a clear demand from other schools for help
with this. There are then questions about the extent to which change, to be
effectively introduced, needs to involve everyone in the production of new
materials, and how much that then produces endless reinventions of the
wheel. It would seem that there is still a need for many schools to create their
own curricula and try them out, because we have not yet enough evidence of
the effect on the attitudes and aspirations of young people of a curriculum
developed with the perspective of gender and race equality. The continued
development of the work does depend on the continued enthusiasm and
willingness of teachers to work hard at it. While at the same time within the
authority many other developments are seen as necessary, hopefully the
principles of gender and race equality will be seen as underpinning

everything, and therefore not in competition with other things for time and attention. It has been necessary, and still is, to work on the acceptance of both race and gender as aspects of an equality perspective, not least with those for whom race is a high priority. Tensions exist for those who see work on gender as an easy way for white teachers, particularly women, to avoid dealing with their racism, while men teachers can be accused of concentrating on race issues to avoid confronting their sexism.

The strategies used within the authority described are intended to produce real change. The evidence for that will be many years in coming. Whether all the necessary conditions for far-reaching change will continue, whether as the effects of initial changes become more obvious the forces of reaction will become organized to resist, whether it is possible to remove patriarchy through education, all remain to be seen.

REFERENCES

Byrne, E.M., *Women and Education*, Tavistock Publications, London, 1978.
Clarricoates, K. The importance of being earnest...Emma...Tam...Jane; perception and categorisation of gender conformity and gender deviation in primary school, in Deem, R. (ed.), *Schooling For Women's Work*, Routledge & Kegan Paul, London, 1980.
Delamont, S., *Sex Roles and the School*, Methuen, London, 1980.
Department of Education and Science (DES), *Curricular Differences for Boys and Girls*, Survey 21, HMSO, London, 1975.
Spender, D. and Sarah, E. (ed.), *Learning to Lose*, The Women's Press, London, 1980.

10

Changing Schools and Changing Society

some reflections on the Girls Into Science and Technology project

ALISON KELLY

The last ten years have seen a rapid growth in at least three areas of educational activity. A number of explicitly feminist projects have been instituted in schools, both in this country and elsewhere. There is a burgeoning literature on the process of change in schools, looking at factors that render projects successful or unsuccessful and help or hinder the institutionalization of change. And there has been a surge in theoretical work, frequently utilizing reproduction models, which examine the links between schools and society. Yet these three areas have developed largely independently of each other. As Yates (1985) has commented:

> Given the popularity in recent years of various forms of reproduction analysis, it is interesting that there has been very little attempt to interpret the funding of counter-sexism programmes in terms of what this says about dominant social interests. Equally there has been little attempt by those involved in counter-sexist action (including at a theoretical level) to use their belief in this to modify the theorizing about the nature of education as an institution.

In this article I want to begin to fill this gap by reflecting on the experience of one counter-sexist programme, Girls Into Science and Technology (GIST). I am not as familiar with other projects, and in general they have not been evaluated as systematically as GIST, but conversations with other workers in this field suggest that our experiences with GIST were by no means unique.

GIST was an action research project which aimed to encourage more girls to continue with physical science and technical craft subjects when these became optional at school. Children entering eight coeducational comprehensive schools in the Manchester area were exposed to a variety of intervention strategies, including visits to schools by women scientists and technologists; curriculum innovation to develop more 'girl-friendly' science materials; workshops with teachers; classroom observation with feedback to the teacher; and careers information. Two other schools were involved in the project as controls, where attitude testing but no intervention took place. Project evaluation showed that children in the action schools became markedly less willing to endorse sex stereotypes and showed slightly more favourable attitudes towards science than children in control schools. The subject choices of girls in the GIST cohort became somewhat less sex stereotyped than in previous years. However, in an independent evaluation of their reactions, Payne *et al.* (1984) found that the teachers we had been working with generally denied that their behaviour had altered as a result of the project. There was some evidence of shifts in teachers' classroom practices, but these were rather limited. The projects and its results are fully described in the Final Report (Kelly *et al.*, 1984).

The project team were fairly satisfied with the changes in children's attitudes and option choices. We never anticipated that a small project (the total funding would barely have provided one extra teacher for six months in each action school) could produce massive changes in traditional beliefs and practices. However, we do confess to a sense of disappointment in the teachers' reactions, and to a scepticism about the extent to which the innovations which were developed during the life of the project will survive in its absence. Teachers can be seen as a filter through which innovations in school have to pass before they become institutionalized, and it is this question of the teachers' response to GIST that I wish to explore here.

In GIST we believed that if teachers were not convinced of the value of an innovation they could—intentionally or unintentionally—sabotage it. If teachers make the usual assumptions of a patriarchal society (that males are 'normal' and females are different; that what boys do is more interesting and more important than what girls do; that women and men have naturally different roles in life), then this will inevitably show in the hidden curriculum of their classroom interactions. For this reason we put a lot of effort into working with teachers. At the beginning of the project we ran a series of workshops to increase their awareness of the scope of the problem and the research that had been done on it, and to sensitize them to their role in perpetuating sex stereotypes. Throughout the three years that we were working in the schools we took every opportunity to reinforce this message in casual conversations with teachers; we tried to involve them in the design and implementation of the various interventions with the children; and we undertook observation in classrooms so that teachers (who knew what we were looking for) could practise gender-fair interactions and gain some insight into their own behaviour.

Havelock (1975) has identified three models of educational change. First is the research and development model, where strategies are developed in a 'scientific' way and then applied, essentially unchanged, in the schools; second is the social interaction model where teachers become aware that other teachers are using new methods and decide to innovate themselves; and third is the problem solving approach where teachers develop strategies to solve a problem they perceive in their own classroom. Although few projects fall neatly into any one category, it seems that for success a large component of problem solving is essential. If teachers are solving their own problems they are typically much more involved in the work and so more likely to sustain their interest over the inevitable difficulties. Chin and Benne (1969) and Hoyle (1970) use a somewhat different typology, which includes the important dimension of power-coercion, evident whenever the law, the LEA or the head teacher mandates a change. However, both articles stress the importance of normative re-educative strategies—by which they mean that teachers must be helped consciously to re-examine their own assumptions and values. They argue that if this is not done then innovations are unlikely to become an integral part of a school system, even if they are formally adopted.

GIST contained many of the features recommended for successful innovation (Berman and McLaughlin, 1978). The project was based around solving a problem (girls' under-representation in optional science classes); staff training was continuous; practitioners were involved in the design of the project which was adapted in the light of experience as it proceeded; the school was treated as a social organization and the support of the head teacher and senior staff was enlisted. Our approach was a mixture of problem-solving and research and development. Teachers were supposed to work out their own solutions to the problem of girls' underrepresentation in science, but the project team provided some suggestions based on the results of previous research. There was also a normative re-educative component as we gently tried to encourage teachers to consider their own behaviour in class.

The main drawback to this approach was that, by and large, the teachers did not see girls' underrepresentation in science as a problem. Nor were they willing to re-examine their own values. Most teachers readily agreed that equality was important, but thought that it already existed, and that any residual differences between girls and boys were genetic. Since they did not accept that there was any sex stereotyping in their classrooms, many teachers did not see the problem as theirs, and did not feel motivated to search for solutions. However we tried to disguise it, the message to teachers was that they had been disadvantaging half their pupils all their professional lives. This is clearly an uncomfortable message to hear. It may account for the distancing techniques employed by so many who, while admitting that it existed elsewhere, insisted that there was no problem in their school.

The Ford Teaching Project, faced with the same dilemma of how to make a situation problematic for teachers, developed techniques of triangulation—collecting and comparing accounts of the lesson from teacher, pupils, observer and tape recorder—to examine classroom processes (Adams, 1980). This took a lot of time and energy, but seems to have been successful in enabling teachers to see the discrepancies between their ideals and the reality of their classrooms. A somewhat similar technique was used in GIST in the classroom observation sessions. This was extremely revealing. However, many of the sex differentiated interactions that we observed originated not with the teacher but with the pupil. So this technique did not dispense with the genetic argument; nor did it demonstrate how different techniques of classroom management could have structured the interactions differently. Teachers remained unwilling to see their own part in either the problem or the solution.

All innovation in schools involves, at least implicitly, a critique of teachers' previous practice, and is thus potentially threatening. However, most projects are concerned with pedagogy, the central purpose of the classroom, and are therefore seen as legitimate areas of concern. However, gender roles extend beyond the school gates, and intervention in this area may be particularly fraught. Many teachers made the link between what we were saying about girls in school and the position of women in their own families—as evidenced by the number of anecdotes we were told about wives and daughters who were either completely happy in their traditional role or had broken into non-traditional fields with no trouble at all. We were thus perceived as criticizing teachers' personal lives as well as their professional practices. This may have made them particularly reluctant to admit that there was a problem at all.

In an attempt to minimize this threatening aspect of the project, we deliberately played down the personal ramifications of sex stereotyping and concentrated on professional concerns of equality of opportunity within schools for all pupils. We didn't talk much about women's inferior position in society and how this is perpetuated through the schools. We hoped that this approach would allow the teachers (most of whom were men) to co-operate with the project without having to re-examine their personal lives and ask themselves questions such as whether it was fair for their wives to have the main responsibility for child care. We used the impersonal authority of research results to substantiate our analysis of the problem and our suggestions for action.

In the short run this worked. We encountered no overt hostility, and most teachers were willing to try out the ideas that we proposed. Perhaps a typical reaction from a (male) science teacher was for an initial scepticism to change gradually into endorsement and even enthusiasm over the first couple of years of the project's work in schools, as it became evident that we had practical ideas and could implement them efficiently. In some cases this enthusiasm waned as the project progressed and the teachers began to realize the enormity of the problem and of the changes required of them and of society in general. But at no stage did anyone formally withdraw from the project.

However, in the long run this purely professional approach may have backfired. Most teachers did not make the links between their own assumptions and girls' underachievement. They didn't examine their own prejudices and motivations and generally remained accepting of the project rather than committed to it. Payne *et al.* found that only four teachers out of the 34 interviewed gave changing teachers' attitudes or behaviours as an aim of the project, and only one mentioned changing women's position in society. The evaluators conclude that 'the project was largely viewed as interventionist in the lives of pupils rather than the lives of teachers'.

The whole process of involving the teachers in the project might have been facilitated if we had set up GIST committees within each school. This idea was discussed, but initially it would have created more work both for us and for the teachers, and it seemed easier to liaise with individual teachers. With hindsight it is clear that such committees could have served to focus a school's activities and give teachers real involvement with and control over the interventions. School committees might also have been a way of increasing the involvement of the feminist teachers who existed in most if not all schools, but were frequently located in the English or social studies departments and had little direct contact with the project. A project newsletter might also have helped teachers to identify with GIST by creating links between schools and sharing information and ideas.

However, involving teachers is not necessarily an advantage to a project. In an interesting report on the Teacher Corps project in the United States (which aimed to improve education for underprivileged children by a special training system for new teachers who would then act as change agents in ghetto schools) Corwin concludes that:

> Contrary to a widely held opinion, broad-based participation did not assure that the program would be successful. Where power was equalised, less technological change occurred, apparently because teachers were in a better position to coopt the program and to use it for their own purposes. Power equalisation facilitates change only if all parties involved agree that change is necessary or desirable.

On the other hand, where existing teachers were not fully involved in developing the programme the new teachers tended to be stigmatized as impractical radicals whose ideas were rejected out of hand.

This stigmatization also seemed to happen on the GIST project. To an extent that surprised us when we read it, the independent evaluation revealed that the project teachers saw the three female members of the project team as *extremely* feminist. Despite our efforts to play down the political content of the project, and a constant feeling that we were biting our tongues off to avoid antagonizing teachers, we were perceived as aggressive and pushy. Interestingly the one male member of the team was seen as much more reasonable, although we felt that his approach was similar to ours. There is thus a real dilemma. If teachers are involved in planning the project, but do not truly share its aims, it may become co-opted and lose all impact; if teachers are not involved in planning they may reject the project as being too radical and impractical.

One way out of this dilemma may be to emphasize the normative re-educative strategy more directly by approaching teachers on a personal as well as a professional level. Since even a muted approach is seen as unacceptably radical, and yet the softly-softly approach produces little change, it may be better to challenge stereotyped behaviour directly. At the risk of alienating some teachers completely, this approach may also enable others to examine the real issues involved in counter-sexist education. This argument is supported by the fact that those teachers who were most effective on the project were mainly either feminists or living with feminists. These were people who had already examined their own lives and made a personal commitment to changing women's position. They were sometimes unsure what form this commitment should take in the classroom, and GIST could be useful in providing suggestions and support.

In retrospect, it seems that we may have given ourselves an impossible task in working with teachers who were not initially convinced of the aims of the project. We wanted to show what could be done with ordinary teachers in ordinary schools. Perhaps the answer is: very little, directly.

But this is not a counsel of despair. Paradoxically, it seems that GIST may have been more effective in other schools than we were in the project schools. The project received considerable publicity, and many teachers in other schools wrote to us requesting copies of our publications or help with particular problems. If teachers are sufficiently interested to take the time to write to us, the chances are that they have already made some of the crucial personal-professional links. GIST could then assist by suggesting what action to take. Moreover, the existence of a funded project could help to legitimize the concern of teachers elsewhere. Girls' underrepresentation in science is now considered a serious educational issue, to an extent that seemed inconceivable five years ago, and GIST has contributed to creating the current awareness. Another way out of the dilemma of working with sceptical teachers may be to concentrate on creating a social climate which demands change in current practices.

What, if anything, does our experience with GIST tell us about the relationship between schooling and society? Most of the currently dominant frameworks for analysing this relationship make use of Marxist or neo-Marxist theories. Clearly one way in which the funding of counter-sexist programmes could be fitted into this framework is by perceiving them purely as legitimating devices. As Yates (1985) says:

'Equal Opportunity' funds, units, appointees can be and are used by those in power to claim that fair treatment is now in operation, hiding the more subtle and diffuse processes of discrimination and alienation that continue.

On this view, publicly funded projects such as GIST, DASI (Developing Anti-Sexist Innovations), and the Schools Council network and equal opportunity advisers in places like ILEA, Brent and Clywd are no more than a smoke screen thrown up by the patriarchal state to disguise its real intentions.

In neoclassical Marxist theory the school is an Ideological State Apparatus (Althusser, 1971) which socializes workers to take their allotted place in a capitalist (and patriarchal) labour market. Although schools have some apparent freedom to change features of their own organization, the situation is in fact 'overdetermined' and changes within schools have little if any impact on society at large. Any change in one direction will be balanced and compensated for by other changes. With respect to girls in science and technology, this argument suggests that GIST could not hope to achieve any real changes because of all the countervailing pressures. Children come to school with their own preconceptions; parents and employers expect the school to do certain things and not others. Even when changes are made within the school in factors such as teaching style or curriculum materials, their effect will be nullified by counterbalancing changes such as boys' reactions or new forms of assessment.

Cultural reproduction theories such as those developed by Paul Willis (1977) put it rather differently. It is not the present situation which is statically replicated; rather the relations between groups are reproduced as their culture is actively recreated, often in new forms. Applied to the present issue, this approach would suggest that changes could occur so that an interest in science and technology became an acceptable part of adolescent female culture. However, this need not affect the patriarchal relations of dominance and subordination between males and females. Even if girls gain qualifications in science and technology, this will not guarantee them jobs in this field, or power and influence in a technological world. Qualified women may be used to fill lower level technician posts, or operate computerized machinery, without affecting male-female hierarchies in society.

Some feminists obviously share these viewpoints—if not the theory underlying them—and have drawn the conclusion that since schools necessarily reproduce patriarchal power structures we should not waste our energy in trying to change them. However, a considerable number of feminists continue to put energy into schools, and unless we are all suffering from a bad case of false consciousness there must be another theory of school-society links at least implicit in our actions. To quote Yates again, the

rhetoric under which education operates, the liberal aims put out by schools in their curriculum statements, the concerns for developing the individual students held by individual teachers, are not of no consequence. Although these ways of seeing the situation may serve to disguise real sources of discrimination, they also to some extent direct practice, and they offer the possibility of being taken up by those dissatisfied with current processes to force some re-direction of them.

Yates reminds us that we should not neglect the overt curriculum, which she sees as a

conscious interruption in the formation of individual identity, one which embodies explicit consideration of the direction towards which the society should move (emphasis in original).

Other authors put more emphasis on changing the 'hidden curriculum' by talking of a school 'ethos' (Rutter *et al.*, 1979) or a 'transformative' school (Reynolds, 1983). These terms embody the idea that the school—rather than the society or the individual—can be the unit of change. By changing the atmosphere or ethos of the school, the attitudes and opportunities of the children within it can be altered. These children with their new outlook, can then alter the society of which they are a part.

The GIST project began with an implicit model of a 'transformative' school. By collaborating with teachers we hoped to produce a school atmosphere with a strong emphasis on equality between the sexes and widening girls' opportunities. If young people left school with these commitments it might affect the reproduction of gender relations in their children and in society as a whole. If a substantial proportion of girls gained qualifications in science and technology they would at least be qualified for jobs in these areas, and so might begin to challenge patriarchal practices. Obviously we did not expect all this to result from one small project. But the theory of working for social change within schools is premissed on the belief that schools can affect society.

In the light of the GIST experience, I would now want to modify this model somewhat. It is difficult if not impossible for researchers to make a school 'transformative'. A school ethos is something that has to grow slowly over a long period, and stem from a deep commitment on the part of heads and teachers. When such a commitment exists it may be possible for researchers to suggest practicable ways to manifest it. This seemed to happen in one of the GIST schools which had a long-standing policy of anti-racist and anti-sexist schooling and a strong group of feminist teachers on the staff. The general atmosphere in the school was distinctly macho and option choices in previous years were strongly sex stereotyped. This school showed more change in subject choices than any other, and it seems likely that the practical ideas and support offered by GIST acted as a catalyst to bring about change where conditions were already favourable.

However, this was not the only effect of the GIST project. Spin-offs into other schools may have been equally important, and this suggests another version of the transformative school through action research hypothesis. Teachers in other schools hear what is going on in the action schools, and feel that this meets some of their own needs. They may in fact have an inflated picture of what is going on in the action schools, but that does not matter. It is the perception of action which is powerful. Publicity about the research project brings the problem into the public eye, and leads other teachers to define it as their problem. This reflects back into the original school, where teachers now feel that they are receiving recognition for something that was previously considered an imposition. Schools which are not involved begin to think that they are behind the times, and decide to set up committees to consider the problem. The method of educational change that this argument suggests is social interaction.

This model describes a feedback between schools and society—what schools provide is influenced by the rhetorical demands placed upon them by society; and these rhetorical demands in turn are influenced by society's perception of what schools are doing. This almost Durkheimian view may be unfashionable, but it seems to provide the most accurate account of what happened in the GIST project. And it has practical implications. Rather than being a nuisance, which distracts one from the important business of work in the schools, publicity becomes an essential element of action research. People need to be made aware of serious educational issues and to know that something can be, and is being, done about them. This does not mean that the project should become mere hype. On the contrary I feel that publicity stunts, such as Women in Science and Engineering (WISE) year, run the risk of trivializing the whole issue by making it appear that all that is needed is a conference and goodwill. It is essential to grapple with the real obstacles involved. In this respect an awareness of the overdetermination argument helps guard against a facile optimism about the power of schools and a corresponding pessimism if the hoped for changes fail to materialize (as was evident with the compensatory education projects of the 1960s). But it is also essential that people elsewhere know what is happening.

ACKNOWLEDGEMENTS

GIST was jointly directed by Judith Whyte and myself; Barbara Smail and John Catton worked with us as schools liaison officers. The project was financed by grants from the Equal Opportunities Commission, the Social Science Research Council, the Schools Council, the Department of Industry Education Unit and Shell U.K. Ltd. The views expressed in this article are not necessarily shared by the other members of the team, or by our sponsors. The Final Report on the project may be obtained by sending a large s.a.e. and £1 to GIST, Department of Sociology, University of Manchester.

REFERENCES

Adams, E. Ford, Teaching Project, in Stenhouse, L. (ed.), *Curriculum Research and Development in Action*, Heinemann, London, 1980.

Althusser, L., Ideology and ideological state apparatuses, in *Lenin and Philosophy and Other Essays*, New Left Books, London, 1971.

Berman, P. and McLaughlin, M.W., *Federal Programs Supporting Educational Change*, Vol. VIII: *Implementing and Sustaining Innovations*, Rand R-1589/8-HEW, May 1978, Santa Monica, California.

Chin, R. and Benne, K.D., General strategies for effecting change in human systems, in Bennis, W.F., Benne K.D. and Chin, R. (eds.), *The Planning of Change*, Holt, Rinehart & Winston, New York, 1969.

Corwin, R.G., *Reform and Organizational Survival: The Teacher Corps as an Instrument of Educational Change*, Wiley, 1973.

Havelock, R.G., The utilization of educational research and development, in Harris, A., Lawn, M. and Prescott, W. (eds.), *Curriculum Innovation*, Croom Helm, London, 1975.

Hoyle, E., Planned organisational change in education, *Research in Education*, Vol. 3, pp. 1–22, 1970.

Kelly, A., Whyte, J. and Smail, B., *Girls Into Science and Technology: Final Report*, Department of Sociology, University of Manchester, 1984.

Payne, G., Hustler, D. and Cuff, T., *GIST or PIST: Teachers' Perceptions of the Project Girls Into Science and Technology*, Manchester Polytechnic, 1984.

Reynolds, D., Paper presented at Sociology of Education conference, Westhill, January 1984.

Rutter, M., Maughan, B. and Ousten, J., with Smith, A., *Fifteen Thousand Hours*, Open Books, London, 1979.

Willis, P., *Learning to Labour*, Saxon House, Farnborough, 1977.

Yates, L., Curriculum becomes our way of contradicting biology and culture: an outline of some dilemmas for non-sexist education, *Australian Journal of Education*, 1985.

Index